Prophetic Preaching
A New Approach

❖❖❖

Prophetic Preaching
A New Approach

OTTO J. BAAB

ABINGDON PRESS
NEW YORK • NASHVILLE

PROPHETIC PREACHING: A NEW APPROACH

Copyright © MCMLVIII by Abingdon Press

Library of Congress Catalog Card Number: 58-6590

SET UP, PRINTED, AND BOUND BY THE
PARTHENON PRESS, AT NASHVILLE,
TENNESSEE, UNITED STATES OF AMERICA

TO MY DAUGHTER MARY

Introduction

THERE IS A WISTFUL LONGING ON THE PART OF PREACHERS TO know the true meaning of prophetic preaching. There is, however, general confusion when it comes to agreement as to its nature and form. To meet that longing and to dispel some of that confusion is the hope of this book.

This book is written by a teacher of preachers for preachers who long to be true prophets of God. This is not a book of prophetic sermons or sermon outlines for those who are unwilling to undergo the intellectual and spiritual discipline which is required for truly effective preaching. It is rather intended for the preacher who seeks to discover a source of power and effectiveness which will manifest itself in the pulpit.

A word is in order as to the present writer's personal attitude toward the Bible and toward the prophets in particular. Continued use and study of the Bible in the classroom and pulpit, in the lecture hall and for more personal purposes, has produced a deep conviction about its place in the faith and life of the Christian community. The Bible is the unique and unrepeatable record of God's purpose and will to establish on earth and in heaven a society of redeemed men and women, dedicated to their Savior and viewing one another with love. The Bible contains both the Word of this purpose and the manner of its communication and accomplishment. For this reason the Bible is essential to salvation. As far as the Old Testament is concerned, this Word is the prophetic Word communicated by the Redeemer through the prophets.

To announce the Word which God has made known and which is recorded in Scripture is still the outstanding obligation of the man of God. Administrative skill, psychological insight, social leadership, priestly proficiency, educational effectiveness, and expertness in human relations are extremely valuable aids. Yet without the effective proclamation of the divine Word, they may become useless and even totally irrelevant to the preacher's task.

It will be enough to point out here that the very nature of the Christian gospel, of which the Church is both product and custodian, centers in the good news of redemption. The recital of this good news is therefore indispensable before anything can happen in the realm of counseling and education. Through the report of the wonderful deeds of God the Church came into being. When men heard the news which culminated in the event of Christ, it was ratified by the Spirit in their own hearts. They became new creatures, filled with power and hope. The activity of the Spirit enabled them to accept the Word of their salvation. These early Christians let this Word penetrate and permeate every dimension of their existence with cleansing and vivifying power. To preach the Word was, and is, the paramount demand upon ministers of Jesus Christ. For this there is still no substitute, unless one rejects the essence of the gospel itself.

When the various stages of the Hebrew prophets' preaching are brought under scrutiny, the modern preacher will sense a spiritual kinship with biblical times. He will find himself faced with a tremendous opportunity and challenge. He will be overwhelmed with preaching insights and ideas, for the prophets are spokesmen of the eternal God. God's righteous love addresses itself to every conceivable human situation with authority and peculiar relevance. When the study of God's spokesman is sincere and imaginative, he will enter his pulpit to communicate the prophet's divine passion for the Word of the Lord to his congregation. This is the glory of prophetic preaching.

OTTO J. BAAB

Contents

I

The Prophetic Preacher's Passion

POPULAR BELIEF VIEWS THE PROPHETS OF ISRAEL AS FIERCE and forbidding individuals, fiery and at times even ferocious in their stern attacks upon existing evils. This view is certainly justified on the basis of a study of the prophets' language. Their choice selection of short, pungent, arresting words and the emotional manner of their speeches is revealed in their writings. One can almost hear the sob of a tortured soul as Jeremiah cries out about the nation's scornful rejection of Israel's God:

> My anguish, my anguish! I writhe in pain!
> Oh, the walls of my heart!
> My heart is beating wildly;
> I cannot keep silent. (4:19.)

The prophetic mood was certainly not one of still waters flowing quietly through green pastures. It was rather like the sudden, roaring, tumultuous stream rushing down a wadi and sweeping all before it in its fury. The prophets were men of deep conviction and of strong passion. They found it impossible to mince words with logical nicety or to be dispassionately objective when they preached or delivered their oracles. Theirs was a singlehearted devotion which moved them intensely,

13

profoundly affecting their spoken words. They were supremely dedicated men, possessed men.

Without this passion the prophets would have ceased to be prophets, so characteristic was it of their life and thought. To discover the nature of this passion, to determine its source, its form, its social and personal direction, and its relation to the prophets' preaching is the purpose of the present chapter. If this inquiry is successful, it should be possible to show how the experience of the great prophets can be utilized by the modern minister. With their experience he can assess his own spiritual commitment and evaluate his own preaching.

In well-known instances this passion appears to have had its origin in the initial call of the prophet. This crucial experience was evidently vividly remembered by the prophets Isaiah, Jeremiah, and Ezekiel. Amos, Hosea, and Micah also seem to point to this experience although the data are not so clear with respect to them. For some of the prophets there is no dependable information on the matter of a call, although we may presuppose it in some cases. This phase of the prophet's life is particularly important for it goes to the root of the prophetic preacher's motivation for his task. The call to prophesy is clearly parallel to the call to preach in the careers of present-day ministers. Our aim is a simple one—the identification of the key features in the call experience. These clues will help us to comprehend the dimensions of the prophet's devotion and of his passionate dedication to his work as spokesman and proclaimer of the Word of God. Our major concern now is to provide an effective description of typical prophetic preaching as it is found in the Bible. This we will undertake for the sake of men now in the ministry who have somehow missed this remarkable biblical phenomenon or who have previously passed it by as meaningless.

14

The great prophets were convinced that they had been called by the God of Israel. They were certain that their prophetic careers were furthered by the active intervention of the Lord of history, the self-revealed Redeemer of Israel. God had specifically summoned them to embark upon an often repugnant career of prophecy to a stubborn nation. Amos explained his activity in Bethel by stating that the Lord had taken him from his work as herdsman and dresser of sycamore-fig trees to be his prophet, although he rejected the title of prophet for reasons mentioned below. Amos was sensitive to national sins. He was grieved by the injustices under which the poor and underprivileged writhed. He was convinced that God would not suffer the rebellion of his people any longer, so he answered the divine summons and went to Bethel and perhaps even to Samaria. What else could he do?

> The lion has roared;
>   who will not fear?
> The Lord God has spoken;
>   who can but prophesy? (3:8.)

God's call was irresistible.

Isaiah recounts how his call came when he was in the temple, perhaps on the occasion of national mourning over the death of Judah's king, Uzziah. Here he was overcome by a sense of the overwhelming holiness of God and had no answer to give except to lament his unworthiness and uncleanness. But when the direct question came, "Whom shall I send?" he was ready with the words, "Here I am! Send me." (6:8.) Awe, indecision, doubt, and self-deprecation were banished when Isaiah sensed the glorious and commanding majesty of the God who called him. He knew full well the danger and complexity of the mis-

15

sion upon which he would embark. As a leading citizen in Jerusalem, a relative of the royal family, Isaiah was conscious of the ominous rise of the power of mighty Assyria and of its threat to Judah's security and independence. In this clear knowledge he nonetheless accepted the divine summons to prophetic action.

And there was Micah—peasant farmer, rugged, bold, forthright, champion of the oppressed, opponent of the trend toward larger farms and foe of absentee landlords (2:2). He opposed those who wielded unscrupulous economic and political power in order to crush the poor without compassion. His was a holy anger against the pseudo religionists who championed nothing except the satisfaction of their appetites. He loosed a righteous wrath against the nation's insensitivity to widespread evil. It was a supernatural wrath which Micah was compelled to identify with God acting in him.

> But as for me, I am filled with power,
>   with the Spirit of the Lord,
>   and with justice and might,
> to declare to Jacob his transgression
>   and to Israel his sin. (3:8.)

God had called him. God had directed him in his course and empowered him to be a prophet. To God's purposes the prophet was passionately committed.

Hosea was distraught by the gross sensuality which flaunted itself as a religion. To him with inescapable clarity there came the divine command to act by entering into a monstrous marriage. Hosea demonstrated in his life and in his words his protest against the nation's idolatrous licentiousness and his own dedication to the one God of righteous love: "And the

16

Lord said to me, 'Go again, love a woman who is beloved of a paramour and is an adulteress.' " (3:1.)

Possibly the youngest of them all when the call came was Jeremiah. He too had the misfortune to live at a time when the struggle of empires threatened the very existence of the small nations like Judah. The Lord called this young man when he was about eighteen years of age and commanded him to be a prophet to the nations! In spite of Jeremiah's protest and excuses, he accepted his terrible burden. He began the career which was so fraught with pain and sorrow and frustration that men compared Jeremiah with the Man of Galilee.

We must also name Ezekiel, strange combination of prophet, priest, seer, statesman, and poet. He too came face to face with the Eternal, succumbed to God's glorious majesty, and accepted the destiny to which he was called. So among the hills, in the city, on the farm, and in the temple the call of the Most High came to the individual prophet. It effectively summoned him to do God's bidding as a preacher of the ruthless Word of man's sin and the compassionate Word of man's deliverance. The summons came in various ways and places, but it came!

The fact of the call has significance to the prophets because of its origin in an act of God. These men did not answer the call of duty or of conscience, the call of country or of community. They responded to the call of God, the God of their fathers, the God of their nation and of its history. This fact alone explains their peculiar passion and their program of preaching in perilous times. It stands in sharp contrast to much that is piously and politely described as a "call" today. What is now often simply one's choice of a career or submission to social pressure appears feeble alongside the prophet's call. He was deeply convinced that it came directly and decisively from God. The prophets thought, and believed, and preached, under the immediate influence of their view that they had been selected and commissioned for their work by a Power outside themselves. This Power had a conscious purpose in calling them and also the ability to direct them in their activities as preaching prophets. God, who had come to them, was the covenant God who had directed the course of Israel's history. This they believed with heart and mind and soul. The credibility of their prophetic witness is at stake if the validity of this belief is repudiated, so conspicuous is its place in everything the prophets did and said.

Aside from the valid evidence for regarding the Bible as authoritative for Christian faith and life, the fact that God did truly call his prophets is fully demonstrated by the integrity of their lives, the consistency of their teachings, and the congruity of their message with the gospel in both Testaments. Without laboring this point, we may briefly consider it. In the prophetic books one can find no trace of self-delusion and fanaticism. In fact self-delusion comes under frequent attack, as can be seen in their bitter condemnation of the "false" prophets. Indeed such elements would be conspicuously out of place in the prophetic records of courageous loyalty to divine truth and sturdy resistance to human pressures. Theirs was a stubborn and steadfast promulgation by word and by life of the message which they had received. They were men who had been made whole by their consuming passion for God. They were wholly given to the work of speaking his Word, and this they did with amazing consistency and historical relevancy. By the flame of their devotion they were fused into oneness with the Word they agonizingly preached. For this task they lived, and for it they died.

The authenticity of the prophet's call is further assured by the close kinship of the prophetic message with the very heart of the Bible's faith and doctrine. The revelation to the prophet of the meaning of God was involved in the call itself. This revelation gave theological substance to the Word that the prophet was called to preach and vitality to the contribution he made to the biblical revelation itself. Through the call the prophet's varied cultural and religious experiences were vividly illuminated by his confrontation with the living God of biblical faith. In this manner what had been traditional became personal. What had been general became particular, centering in the prophet's will and heart as he radically affirmed the meaning of God for his own life. In effect, this was a new revelation to the prophet by which he was moved to impart to his people the true knowledge of God. What had thus been revealed to him was in fundamental agreement with the entire biblical faith and outlook.

In the prophet's call there were three elements, none of which can be disregarded. The first and greatest of these, of course, was the activity of God. The other two were closely related—the life and character of the individual prophet and the fact of his community. If God was the source and determiner of the prophet's call, the community was its object. The prophet stood between God and the community, receiving from the former what he was to give the latter.

The basic nature of the call suggests how far it was removed from a purely private, subjective experience. It also suggests the dimensions of the passion which the call aroused in the soul of the prophet. The call shook his soul as it reached to the depth of his being. It searched out his secret sins and evoked his noblest capacities in responding to it. The prophet cried, "Woe is me! . . . I am a man of unclean lips," when the call came. Yet he accepted it with the assurance that God would enable his voice and his words to be adequate to his need. He received the courage to keep on preaching even when his listeners became increasingly unresponsive. His call awakened the full devotion of his heart and the complete commitment of his manhood to the performance of the prophetic function. So it was a personal passion which possessed the prophet.

At this point modern readers sense the strangeness of these men of God—such prized values as love, marriage, economic or professional ambition, citizenship, and the like seem unimportant to the prophets. These values were not ignored, but they were subordinated to the prophet's dominant concern for the divine Word. This divine Word he must proclaim, no matter what the cost. The passion was peculiarly *his,* of course, but its object and range went far beyond personal feeling and interest. The call and the passion it engendered had a social purpose and direction. It was not simply a "wonderful experience" which began with God and ended with the prophet. On the contrary, its fulfillment was possible only in relation to the community called Israel. This community was the destination of the prophetic Word even as its redemption through judgment and mercy was the purpose of the prophet's preaching.

This third aspect of the call merits our attention as we try to understand the passion of the prophet. This passion was stimulated and channeled by the prophet's sense of belonging to this community. The community in turn belonged to his God. So the prophet was torn by alternating anger and love as he contemplated first the destructive evil in the community and then its divine possibilities through obedience to God. He preached to a people which he loved as only a Hebrew steeped in its splendid history and heroic traditions can love. He preached against the people of his love as only a man consumed with the fires of God's justice can preach when faced with cruelty and iniquity.

No wonder the prophet was torn and stricken. He clearly saw the shortcomings and injustices of the faithless people chosen to be the beloved of the Most High. With tears of anger and pity he pleaded with this people to return to its God for needed forgiveness and deliverance from evil. He was a man of tension and strife, forced to oppose his people that God might save them. He had to cry out:

> My grief is beyond healing,
>   my heart is sick within me. (Jer. 8:18.)
>
> . . . .
>
> Why did I come forth from the womb
>   to see toil and sorrow? (Jer. 20:18.)

It is evident that the prophet's unrest and grief were caused by his people's sin against their God. To this God the prophet had surrendered himself fully. The source of his deep feeling was therefore God himself. God had called him and confronted him with the intolerable dilemma of denying his human impulses and speaking the word of doom with the voice of God. Nothing could stand in the way of the declaration of God's Word and the pronouncement of his will—neither principalities nor powers of earth or of the dark places under the earth could prevent his fulfillment of his divinely determined ministry of preaching. Only through such absolute obedience to the divine command to preach can the prophet know that he has succeeded. The very nature of the prophet's call to declare God's Word established this as the only conceivable basis for evaluating his achievement. Absolute obedience to God's purpose for him was the only obedience which he could consider.

This passion for God had a characteristic form which distinguished it from other types of love for God in the history of religions. The intense ecstasy of certain experiences in which the mystic has an indescribable and ineffable feeling of supreme bliss was not the experience of the prophets. Assuredly a numinous and nonrational element may be found in the books which are associated with their names; but there is no consuming, prostrating, paralyzing passion for God the wholly Other. It is interesting that such absorbing and self-destroying feeling experiences may be especially noticed in certain oriental religions. These have influenced Christian thinking about love for God. Such an unbiblical viewpoint is in sharp contrast to the view of the prophets. For them surrender and submission to God paradoxically arouse forces which produce the highest form of individuality. In his achievement of such true personhood the prophet's passion for his God played a major role. In view of this fact the distinctive quality of the prophet's passion must be sought in the special nature of his God.

The God of Amos, Isaiah, and Jeremiah was not a universal absolute, devotion to which (rather than whom) annihilated personality. On the contrary the God of Amos, Isaiah, and Jeremiah was the holy Creator-Redeemer, at work in a world of moral freedom for the purpose of producing in a dedicated community a society of persons bound together by a common Spirit. This redeemed society was to be marked by obedience to the God of its salvation. The prophet who preached the Word of such a God adored him through the assertion of his full manhood, not through its suppression.

It was not some unknowable being which inflamed the prophet. The righteous, merciful, covenant God had revealed himself in history and issued a mandate to his spokesmen to declare his Word of life and truth. This covenant God was made known at Sinai and in acts of deliverance in the life of the nation. The God of prophetic passion held before men the potentialities of eternal good or of eternal disaster, depending upon their obedient love of their Redeemer or their defiant desertion of his cause and purpose for them. No wonder that the prophets gave themselves with such vigor and intensity of feeling to their God. He who made the earth and the heavens, who created man in his own image, who determined the course of man's history, now upheld man's choice of goodness and condemned his choice of wrongdoing.

It is the self-disclosure of this God that determined the unique form of the prophet's allegiance and commitment. His passionate orientation toward God had a moral force, a social direction, and a personal depth which cannot be seen in non-prophetic types of religious behavior. The prophet's passion for God was an ethical passion directed to the God of transcendent righteousness. In comparison all other moralities shrank into insignificance. Justice, righteousness, integrity, honor, kindness, compassion, and neighborliness are not abstract propositions in ethics. They are symbols of the will and nature of the eternal Redeemer of men. They are indications, impelling and enthralling, of the beauty of his holiness. These prophets did not know or care about morality as such; they knew and cared supremely about the God of ultimate mercy and justice.

All this had its effect. When the prophets encountered tyranny in the government or corruption in the market place, they were provoked to passionate speech as no other group of men has ever been provoked. They saw social evil in relation to the righteous, compassionate God to whom they had given the full measure of devotion. Where men were debased and disgraced by the evil that other men did, the problem ceased to be simply a matter of reordering society: it related actually to God's purposes as the Savior of his people. So the prophet, ancient or modern, is much more than a champion of his downtrodden fellows. The prophet became in truth the servant of the living God who cannot be glorified save by doing justly and loving mercy in harmony with God's revealed will.

This moral passion which stemmed from devotion to God was neither vague sentimentality nor glorified self-interest. The prophet's conviction was intimately associated with God's revealed demands upon all his people in all their relationships and activities. It inevitably took a social direction. It was oriented toward the society of Israel especially, although it also considered other national and ethnic groups related to her in her history. The prophet preached to this society and worked for its welfare and redemption because it was potentially the redeemed society, the kingdom of God. For the sake of this society God took action in history.

Through this work the prophet revealed more than love of his people. The prophet's love of his people and its institutions was conditioned and qualified by his devotion to God. This made for a very special kind of patriotism, since it was always the will of God which determined the prophet's action and attitude toward national policy. It is one of the astonishing facts of history, unparalleled elsewhere, that the prophets rejected contemporary views of what constituted national interest, defied those in authority, and did so with impunity except for abuse and personal attack on occasion. This phenomenon merits a brief discussion.

The biblical account of the work of Isaiah and Jeremiah readily illustrates their amazing freedom. With forceful words they denounced the nation and its leaders, pulling no punches as they lashed out at rulers, prophets, priests, and so-called wise men. They used such epithets as "sinful nation," "rebels," "sinners," "oppressors," "godless nation," "drunkards," "faithless Israel," "stupid children," "lusty stallions," and "lying sons." And when we search for whole sentences rather than words or phrases, the skill and courage of the prophetic writers in identifying and naming national evil proves to be extraordinary indeed.

Isaiah approached the rulers of Judah (he was active during the reigns of several kings) and gave them pointed warnings concerning the political programs they were instituting. In the name of the God of Israel he enunciated a point of view which to put it moderately, must have seemed to the king as not in harmony with national interest (chs. 7–8). When Jerusalem a century after Isaiah's time was fighting for her very existence against the Babylonian armies, Jeremiah advised desertion to the enemy as the only way of escaping death by the sword. He grimly announced that defense of the city was useless; it would certainly be taken and its defenders be put to the sword or taken into exile. Instead of being immediately executed, the prophet was but briefly imprisoned and then allowed to spread "subversion" and treason once more.

Aside from the difference in attitude toward its prophets held by ancient Judah and by nations today, an additional explanation for Israel's toleration of her disagreeable and dangerous prophets must be sought. This explanation is surely related to the passion of this group of leaders for their fellow Israelites and their nation within the context of their religious faith. Passionate allegiance to God was the basis of their special kind of loyalty to people and nation. Because of this allegiance they were not less but rather more loyal to the community in which they worked. Possibly some realization of this fact aided in protecting the prophets from the anger of the state. A contributing factor almost certainly was the state's memory of its own origin in the permissive action of God through such early prophets as Samuel. The tradition persisted in Israel that God had intended it to be a theocracy rather than an autocracy. So the supreme motive for the work of the prophets was this unqualified surrender to the God who had called them. This constitutes at once the uniqueness and the strangeness of the prophet's commitment and passion.

This absorbing devotion to God did not rule out other human emotions in the life of the prophet. Because he was a prophet, he was no less a man. He felt and reacted to influences in his surroundings. Jeremiah frankly revealed his feelings and moods on several occasions, although the other prophets were almost as candid. He was bitterly angry and deeply hurt over news of the conspiracy by former associates to take his life (12:3; 17:18). He called upon them awful curses from God. He cried out:

> Why is my pain unceasing,
> my wound incurable,
> refusing to be healed? (15:18).

At the time of his call he protested vigorously against God's desire to use him as a prophet to the nations, doubtless realizing the difficulty of interpreting the divine will in the complex international situation that existed in his day.

We also read how Ezekiel suffered in stoic silence on the occasion of the death of his wife (24:15-18). He reported: "At evening my wife died. And on the next morning I did as I was commanded" (that is, refrained from formal mourning and carried on his work as a prophet).

We are moved by the tragedy of Hosea as we hear how the misery of his broken home, caused by the adultery of his wife, brought home to him the lesson of divine forgiveness toward Israel. On the surface and between the lines we see revealed the moods and passions of very human persons, capable of intense hatred, fear, love, and suffering.

What can we say about the relation of these human passions to the supreme passion of God which dominated their lives? Certainly theirs is not a love of God which transformed them into "perfect saints." They were transformed men, yes, but only in the sense that they were possessed of a strong sense of mission which directed them on their course and gave them the power to hold out in the face of doubt and hardships. They were not primarily notable for the sanctity of their lives, as far as available biblical records are concerned, although conclusions from silence may be drawn too far. The Word the prophet voiced was, and is, more important than the details of his personal life. Conflicting desires and motives fought within their souls so that they were destined to be men of sorrow and tension. But even this fate was turned to a good purpose, for it increased the poignant urgency with which they promulgated the Word.

It is clear that the great passion of the prophet was the clue to his power and effectiveness as a preacher of the Word of the gospel. How can this be preserved? Would not the glory of the call wane and its passion diminish under the attrition of the familiar preaching task and the impact of popular ennui or open disapproval? Can the wonder of such an initial experience be retained during the frustrations and disappointments of earnest attempts to secure acceptance of the preached Word? Will the flame that was once kindled continue to burn brightly and steadily? What method did the prophet use to preserve the experience that brought him where he stood as a commissioned and committed man? That the prophet of old had disappointments and disillusionments, there can be no doubt. That he is not alone in this, any preacher of the gospel in this generation will ruefully admit. But unless the glow is kept alive in the heart and strength is constantly renewed by contact with its source, preaching will become a mere chore. "Talking about religion" at stated times is a poor excuse for a stirring, condemning, saving utterance about the Word of God which comes from a man who has an irresistible compulsion to speak. If preaching is to be like that of the early Christians, the preacher's passion for his God cannot be allowed to wane. Then, like them, he will be able to assert: "For we cannot but speak of what we have seen and heard" (Acts 4:20).

I am referring here, of course, to genuine feeling and passion, not to spurious kinds, which may deceive some congregations and even seasoned sermon tasters among them. There are "spirituality" and unction which are neither real nor prophetic in the sense which I am attempting to express. A preacher may generate homiletical "steam" in the pulpit and create a false impression of holy passion by his gestures, his intonation, and his inflection. He may be so successful in creating this impression that he will come to believe it himself. From this vicious circle nothing less than a catastrophe can release him. Such synthetic spirituality may be detected, however, by applying to it the norm of true prophetic feeling. This requires of the prophet a deep-seated devotion to the God of righteous purpose who reveals his desires to men through his prophets as well as through the gift of his Spirit.

The true prophet knows that God wants to use him in defining and producing true community in the world. His entire being is stirred and reorganized around such a purpose so that he may do his part in realizing it. In doing it he will be completely selfless even while he fixes his attention upon the humanly impossible task which has been assigned to him. Such a man is surely in the prophetic succession. If these attitudes are not found in the preacher, we may be sure that either he is deceiving himself or he is deliberately taking the false and easy way of the "lying" prophets who are so bitingly condemned in the Old Testament.

Still the question remains: How can genuine dedication be perpetuated? What do the prophets of old teach those prophets who are living now? The Israelite prophets did not vainly try to secure a repetition of their initial call, as glorious as that had proved to be. There could hardly be more than one inaugural call in their lives. Nonetheless, the reader of their books is impressed by the frequent indications of God's direct participation in their ministry. When in trouble, in doubt, or in pain, or when faced by a baffling problem caused by the state of the nation during a particular crisis, the prophets called upon God. And God replied specifically and pertinently. Theirs was no once-for-all call to which they could look back wistfully as at a cherished memory. It was really a continuing call, affirmed and reaffirmed by the challenge and opportunity of swiftly moving events in their lives, through which and for the interpretation of which God appeared to them in power.

Here then was one way of keeping alive the passion of the prophet—he was ready to discern the work of God at every turn of history, both history completed and history in the making. Through this readiness every moment, every crisis, every decision, encountered by the prophet was the occasion for the renewal of his faith and the rekindling of the fires of his inspired imagination. In his own vocational decision, in the nation's vacillating foreign policy, in a king's immorality, in the branch of an almond tree, in the defeat of the nation, the prophet again and again found the occasion for capturing the glory and the agony of serving as the interpreter of the Word of the living God. All the world of nature and of history be-

29

came a sacramental expression of God's summons to the prophets to follow him in singlehearted allegiance.

By steadfastly reflecting God's purpose, the prophets received a regular access of new power and a continual confirmation of their original dedication to preach prophetically in his name. Their sermons were in themselves instruments of spiritual renewal. The very Word of the Lord which they proclaimed was a revelatory Word, not only to their people but to the prophets themselves. This Word, as it came to and was communicated by them, constantly confronted them with the meaning and wonder of God's action in the history of his people. Every public utterance by the prophet was thus a personal witness to his faith in God as well as a pronouncement of God's will for his people.

The prophetic preacher in this conception of his sermon is a sinner who has learned in his own life the power of God's forgiving love, his call to a new way of life, and the joy of surrender to him. The prophet testifies to what has happened to him through the grace of God. Like the apostles he declares the wonder of what God has done for him: "They . . . spoke the word of God with boldness. . . . With great power the apostles gave their testimony." (Acts 4:31, 33.) He makes known and available to his listeners what has come to him. "I give you what I have," he can say with Peter (Acts 3:6).

This personal relation of the prophet to his sermon revives in the prophet himself a strong sense of God's abiding concern for the effectiveness of his ministry. What prophetic preacher has not experienced this upsurge of confidence and joy in his preaching after putting into it his level best of study and humble submission to the will of God? He realizes then that it is really God who works in him to form and to energize his words. It is also God who brings the Word the preacher sows to full fruition. For such a preacher, as for the prophets, there is no real diminution of the prophetic glow and of the prophetic passion, even though moments and moods of disheartenment do come. By his faithfulness to the Source of his own redemption in his preaching, to adapt the notable words of Habakkuk (2:4), he shall live!

The minister's entire professional and personal life must be viewed as a unified experience. The preachment from the pulpit and the prayer in the privacy of one's room reflect the spiritual integrity of a dedicated man, whose witness to his faith is seen in all his activities and words, although most clearly and forcefully in the well-prepared sermon. Prayer, Bible study, sermon preparation and sermon delivery, as well as the preacher's integrity in community relations, fit together as expressions of a life whose passion is God alone. All that is done derives from and gives support to the preacher's radical devotion to the divine Revealer whose Word he is called to preach.

True prophetic passion provides genuine motivation, deep conviction, compassionate social concern, and challenging authority for preaching the Word. It is the preacher's very life. Without it he is nothing but sounding brass echoing popular platitudes or a tinkling cymbal making pleasant sounds. Without it he communicates no commanding truth to lift men up to God or to reveal them to themselves. This passion indicates both why he must preach and what he must preach. It marks his call as well as the reason for its coming, for God has commissioned him to preach a special Word to men. And this Word is sure to be preached with power when the prophet deeply experiences the presence of the One who is its source.

II

The Prophetic Preacher's Problem

THE PASSION OF THE PROPHET GIVES HIM THE COURAGE TO FACE
the difficult problems which attend his ministry. The very
nature of prophetic preaching produces problems for the
preacher and for his people. The prophet's people and the world
of ideas and practices in which they live are a problem to
him. It is evident from the experience of the prophets of Israel
that true adjustment to the prophetic calling meant painful
maladjustment to their human environment. This is in striking
contrast to the effort of many modern preachers and pastors to
produce for themselves and for their people that harmony with
their surroundings which will bring peace and poise.

In the lives of the prophets may be seen evidences of severe
conflict, persecution, and even martyrdom as the result of their
condemnation of the contemporary culture and even of organized religion. Both Testaments make a strong plea to men of
God: "Do not be conformed to this world." Because of the
Word they were required to proclaim, the prophets had to
oppose whatever stood in the way of their people's acceptance of
its demands.

Strangely enough, this nonconformity to the prophet's world
made him acutely aware of that world and of its great value to

him. He was humanly a participant in the social process, a beneficiary of its numerous values, and an intimate part of his community. He was to an exceptional degree sensitized to its worth and power. His agony was all the greater when the inexorable Word came to him in the form of a demand that he utter violent denunciations against his people and against all that they held dear. Ardently loyal to Israel, the prophet was also passionately loyal to Israel's God. Thus he was caught up in the complicated currents of human history.

He was inescapably enmeshed in the network of community relationships and yet sharply conscious of his painful apartness and of disturbing antagonisms—antagonisms to family, clan, city, and nation. He was a man trapped in history during a period of aggressive and arrogant imperialism, when the armies of Assyria, Egypt, Babylonia, and Persia in succession marched victoriously over his land. He was the citizen of a mean and lowly nation, meagerly equipped with natural or technical resources for stemming the tides of empire which always threatened to engulf her. He lived among a people who compensated for frequent defeats by dreaming of an idealized past or a glorious future. In these circumstances the prophet suffered as a sensitive soul. His pain was greatly intensified when he was required to destroy the false hopes of his people.

The prophet was doomed to announce the imminence of defeat to the citizens of a proud nation. Israel was conscious throughout her history of a peculiar call to a divine destiny, although she was often disastrously blind to the real implications of this destiny. The prophet was a man with the gift of sight and insight. He could neither hide from life nor shut his eyes to external evidences of evil. Nor could he harden his heart to an awareness of the more terrible evil of inner and entrenched sin and rebellion. He was under profound compulsion both to see and to understand the ultimate meaning of all that he saw in the light of destiny and divine judgment.

Called, commanded, and commissioned, the prophet was summoned out of the world although he continued to live in it. He lived with God yet dwelt among men. He shared their emotions and their fears, thought their thoughts and dreamed their dreams. And in addition he bore the crushing burden of a divine hatred for the institutionalized injustice and inhumanity which flaunted God's purposes for his chosen people. The divine wrath which was within him drove him to declare the word of judgment; the divine mercy which God had also implanted in his heart stirred him to declare the possibility of restoration after judgment.

It was God who was working in him, commanding him to preach and to denounce. In the face of this command the prophet found his natural inclination warring against the supernatural demand. He knew no peace. He was a problem to himself and to his people. How could he fulfill his life as a human being and find a measure of contentment under such circumstances? What could a prophet preach to his people so that he might be true to his Lord and at the same time remain in effective rapport with his congregation?

Heavy pressure was brought to bear upon the prophet by his contemporaries. Note, for example, the words used by the people who disliked the brutal candor of the prophet Isaiah. They advised the prophets to speak to them of pleasant matters: "Speak to us smooth things" (Isa. 30:10). Could he have done this, the prophet might have had no problem of tension within himself. The people desired entertaining homilies or an interpretation of faith that might make it a convenient instrument for furthering their own interests.

One notes in this connection the published account of one

prominent preacher's advice to those who are afflicted with a feeling of personal inferiority. Before going in to see the boss about a possible promotion, they should pray so as to take their minds off themselves. Prayer is here placed in the category of sitting on a tack. A tack will also get a man's mind off his coming encounter with the boss! No indication is given here of — prayer as the heart-probing, agonizing baring of the soul to the blazing holiness of the righteous God of the universe who demands confession of sin, repentance, and obedience. Nor did these elements appear in the people's request made to Isaiah and the other true prophets. By popular demand religion is readily debased into a technique among several possible techniques for the cultivation of self-confidence or social success. This was, and is, both the experience and the temptation of prophets who are called of God.

The prophetic preacher of our time lives in the midst of severe cultural conflicts. These conflicts impinge upon him and affect his work as a religious person and a minister. The pressures upon him are certainly not less than those which were exerted upon his ancient predecessors. Conflict is dramatically and painfully felt by the prophetic preacher, even as it was by Hosea, Micah, and Isaiah. Like these men he is imprisoned by implacable and undeniable historical forces which threaten his integrity and endanger his calling. He is caught in a maelstrom of swiftly moving and sometimes contending forces over which he has no effectual control. If he is a true prophet, he must be aware of these forces and evaluate them in relation to the divine power that moves in history and whose meaning he is called upon to declare. How can he do this if he is imprisoned by them?

The influences and currents of thought which characterize the world are always powerful and sometimes menacing to prophetic activity. In our time they have assumed a peculiar and diabolical form which directly opposes them to the demands and sovereign claims of the prophet's God. These evil forces are implemented by vast technological equipment, aggressive and highly self-conscious political systems, and powerful, intellectually arrogant ideologies. Their very aggressiveness and articulate opposition to the God of the preacher-prophet not only demands of him a knowledge of the social and cultural evils which challenge his faith, but even more asks of him the passion and courage to attack them incisively and effectively.

The prophet lives in two worlds—the world of human action and the world of the divine Word and purpose. On the one hand he may be tempted and seduced, as are all men, by a thing-centered, materialistic culture. On the other hand the prophet's God reveals to him the "world's" true nature, as a deadly foe of the life of the spirit and of faith. Yet possession of this insight does not remove the dilemma in which he finds himself. He still longs for a life of peace even while he is compelled to share the wrath and the agony of God at the evil that men do.

The prophet, nonetheless, is compelled to relate himself to his people and to the evils that beset and debase them. His position is in the "midst of the people." Set in their midst, confronted by the need to serve unhesitantly the Lord of history and at the same time to remain close to the congregation, the prophetic preacher does not make it easy for them. The people of such a prophet are caught in a dilemma too. They suffer when they give him freedom of speech, for he lashes and rebukes them with fearless words from the Most High. He arouses slumbering consciences to a painful awareness of their indifference to evil. They also suffer when they suppress him or destroy him. They constantly face the possibility that the evil he would have condemned may yet ruin their civilization and community.

Faced by this dilemma, the people cannot remain indifferent — toward their prophet. Neither can they remain inactive in the face of his faithful performance of his prophetic office. They must do something. Several alternatives are at hand: they may remove him bodily and thus remove the painful tensions which his disagreeable haranguings tend to produce. Or they may slowly destroy him spiritually by cleverly pointing out the relation between salary and "suitable" preaching. His people may deal with him by enduring him unresponsively while at the same time giving him, so they fondly believe, "freedom of the pulpit." In any one of these ways, and in still others, they can find peace as well as release from the discomfort of his presence in the pulpit.

With Amaziah, the advocate of a comforting and tranquilizing gospel, they may say to their modern prophet: "Go to Judah —Middletown—and there eat bread." In language which is more direct, they may say to his distraught bishop: "Transfer him to Theopolis even though it means an increase in salary; get him out of here!" What they mean, of course, paraphrases the words of Micah: "Only the man who prophesies what we like to hear can be our prophet." This is blunt but it suggests the ecclesiastical maneuvering which is used when a prophet becomes too much for his people.

By far the most effective method of disposing of the prophetic preacher is to let him preach his heart out to unresponsive pew occupants. The inhabitants of Jerusalem did this to the prophet Isaiah, if we can so interpret the passage in which he records their reaction to his long ministry:

> "Hear and hear, but do not understand;
> see and see, but do not perceive."

Make the heart of this people fat,
   and their ears heavy,
   and shut their eyes;
lest they see with their eyes,
   and hear with their ears,
and understand with their hearts,
   and turn and be healed. (6:9-10.)

Isaiah here doubtless reported what happened when the people heard his word of judgment and doom. Contemporary use of this technique permits the congregation to point with pride to its "free pulpit" and yet to conduct their affairs as they please. In time impassioned pleas cease to hurt or to move. The liturgies of worship may remain for spiritual edification, even while the sermon is endured. From the standpoint of the preacher-prophet the use of this alternative at least provides an opportunity for prophetic utterance although it may finally drive him to despair.

There is, obviously, another course which the prophet's people may take. They may keep him, encourage him, pray for him, listen to him, and repent of the sins of which his honest and courageous preaching has convicted them. This is the response which God seeks and in which his prophets take delight, although they know full well it will be rare. The way of the Lord is too disturbing, too revolutionary, too humiliating, to be followed by many. The preacher is prone to judge the effectiveness of his work by the influence which he exercises over his people, except when he remembers that he is only an instrument in the hands of God. Then he is reminded that his clear utterance of the divine Word is sufficient, as long as this is done faithfully and meaningfully. The ultimate results are not up to him. He knows that God's success is sure, even though it cannot be measured with man's yardstick.

Paradoxically, the problem of prophetic preaching as it affects the preacher includes the effective communication of the Word from God which relates to judgment and redemption. Such communication is central to the preacher's task. This must not be confused with verbal expression. The books of the prophets indicate that these ancient preachers were greatly interested in proclaiming the Word in such a way as to make it understood. The Word was to be useful as the basis for action by men in the redirection of their wills and in the reformation of their institutions.

This need for tangible results makes the problem of communication all the more acute. How can the preacher bridge the gap between the human and the divine? How can he enable the ways of men to be patterned after the ways of God? How can his furious word of judgment become a word of grace and hope? How can he bring men to repentance and to an understanding of what they must do in their daily lives and social practices to embody the divine will? Such questions cannot be ignored. The striking antagonism of the preached Word toward the cherished customs and beliefs of the people who hear it will not let them rest. Can the prophet who by the nature of his call is set against his people also be *for* his people in an effective way? Can he minister to them even though, or as, he denounces them?

This problem cannot be solved by the easy expedient of adulterating the Word of truth. The prophet is under bond to declare not his own word, but that of his God. On this matter he dare not compromise. The meaning of the Word is self-authenticated and self-communicated when it is heard by men, since they are created with the capacity to hear and to understand it. In Hebrew thought, understanding and knowing the Word is primarily a matter of spiritual discernment through that Spirit which God has given to each man. It is universal in its divine relevance to man's sin and final destiny. The terrible simplicity of judgment, sin, repentance, faith, obedience, is realized by the soul of a man when the Word is preached to him with faithfulness and power. The prophet doesn't need to do any explaining; the Word is its own interpreter.

The Word the prophet proclaims is always a relevant and cogent Word. It is concerned with man's experience of God as *in history* he accepts or rejects the power which is offered for his full salvation. The Word cannot be preached apart from its relationship to this redemption-in-history. The Word comes to the prophet in particular times and places. It must be proclaimed by him to a people in a particular historical milieu. It is thus always a Word which has become flesh, imparted as it is by men to men. Unlike the eternal categories and unchanging ideas of Greek philosophy or the eternal absolutes of moralistic religion, the Word is neither detected nor understood apart from the concrete context of life. This is why the language of the prophets of Israel abounds in allusions to history, to international relations, to family life, to business activities, to national affairs, and to religion in the local community.

Hosea's marriage reflected his account of the divine Word as love. The business trips of Amos to Bethel provided the occasion for his radical pronouncements about the Word as justice in human relations. Isaiah's involvement in international relations talks at Jerusalem convinced him profoundly of the meaning of the Word as faith and loyalty to God. As one reads the prophets, he finds sharp, incisive, penetrating words of spiritual action, puncturing and destroying the illusions by which men tried to live. The prophets replaced these mirages with the fact of the redeeming power of God.

The modern prophet finds that a similar involvement in his world is unavoidable for himself and for his people. He, too, declares and tries to communicate the historical, revealed Word of deliverance and new life. While this word originated in the will of the God of biblical revelation and received its classic expression in terms of Israel's culture and faith, it is nonetheless the most timely word that can be uttered to our generation. Into each problem, situation, relationship, which is peculiar to our time, this divine truth penetrates with illuminating effect, exposing its essential nature and revealing its meaning in the light of God's purpose. For this reason the prophet is bound to be heard. He is more than up to date, since his God is always ahead of history, constituting its goal and directing its course.

For this reason the modern prophet, as his early forerunner, will utter the word both of condemnation and of consolation. Man still needs to know the wrath of God's love and the love of his wrath as these bear upon the problems which so sorely beset him. Such a prophetic preacher will never confuse the issues of his day with the eternal issues of life and death and salvation. Only as current events fit into the grand design of God can they be appropriately treated in the prophetic message. The prophet sees and interprets all things from the standpoint of this design. Prophetic histories in the Old Testament, such as those in the books of Kings, show how the prophet ought to deal with events. Only what relates in their judgment to the nation's compliance or noncompliance with God's will is regarded as worthy of attention. For the prophet the problem of history was the problem of faithfulness to history's God. The solution of this problem demanded bringing the *total life of the community* into line with the divine mercy and justice.

The prophet's communication was retained, even though he often moved far ahead of his people, by the continuous relevance of his words to the human situation. In the most bitter of his tirades against them, they experienced a feeling of his deep concern for their salvation. Through him they felt an awareness of the merciful compassion of God. In the work of the Hebrew prophets one indeed finds little evidence of a pastoral ministry as we know it today, but one does find a theological note without which a pastoral ministry is meaningless. For the total work of the preacher there must be adequate communication of the Word. This communication is the source of the prophet's effectiveness in all that he does. The Word is the instrument by which divine power flows into human life, the method of making healing and help available to men who are distressed in body and spirit, the channel through which the kingdoms and societies of this world may become the kingdom of the Lord.

So the varied problems related to prophetic preaching and to the prophet himself are really one problem. In performing his principal task well, the prophet is obedient to the God for whom he is spokesman. In this obedience he finds peace, although it is not the kind the world gives. He finds also hearers, although some men will turn against him. His preachments chastise and guide, condemn and console, his people as they endure their tragic history. Through the biblical prophets Israel triumphed over misfortune and defeat, emerging as a victorious remnant, a loyal Judaism from which was to arise the Messiah of God in the fullness of time. In the fullness of time God has a reward for the modern prophet as well.

For the prophet's faithfulness in proclaiming the Word he is rewarded by an access of preaching power, a broadening of horizons, a deepening of conviction concerning his ministry and message, and by an enrichment of his program of ministerial activity. Once having solved his greatest problem—that of his main function—he need not worry about the problems that are subordinate to it. To deal with these secondary problems he has new insight, vision, and perspective.

And in this experience of true prophecy the people who hear him are also rewarded, beyond what they can possibly imagine. The prophet's God-given assurance and authority arouse the conviction that his Word is for them. It reveals the true nature and direction of their lives as God alone knows them. They see life whole in a culture which tends to take it, and them, apart in a process of ruinous fragmentation. They are enabled to resist the spiritual disintegration which destroys true manhood and once again may attempt living as sons of the Most High. Their prophet's preaching brings them power as well as truth. With this power they can overcome the world. By it they can find victory even as they seek to witness to the meaning of God's love and justice in their social relations.

This is their reward for hearing their prophet and receiving the Word of his God. When the results of hearing are at work, the problem of unease which their sin creates in the presence of the prophet finds solution once and for all. Together the prophet and his people realize what it means to know that they are God's people. They have been chosen to do God's work in the world according to his Word made manifest in Scripture and in the Word made flesh, even Jesus Christ their Lord.

III

The Prophet's Purpose

THE PROPHET'S PURPOSE IS INTIMATELY RELATED TO HIS BACK-
ground of personal experience in the Israelite community. This
strongly influenced the prophet's conception of his task. We may
distinguish the primary purpose of the prophet from his purposes or goals as he delivers his various addresses. His whole
prophetic career had a clear purpose even as each speech was
associated with a definite objective. Thus we are concerned here
with both the immediate aims and the ultimate goals of the
prophets as preachers. Whether, as we should expect, the two
kinds of purposes are related remains to be seen. Logically they
should be. But the pressures which are exerted upon the modern
minister to deviate from the path of faithfulness to his call
suggest why his professed purpose to be a prophet of God may
not always motivate him in his preaching. This could also have
been the case with the prophets of Israel. In all probability
complete consistency was not any easier for them than it is now.

In their day doubtless many prophets fell by the wayside.
They gave up the struggle to remain true to their calling although they continued to perform in some sense the function of
a prophet. These were included in the category of "false"
prophets which is prominent in the Old Testament, although

some of these were so called because they were associated with a hyphenated Baal-Yahweh religion. But in this classification may have belonged also those prophets who prophesied perfunctorily and spoke for the sake of any personal advantage that might accrue if their listeners were pleased by what was said. These set up objectives for their "sermons" which had little or no relation to the initial experience of a call. Their ultimate purpose was success and power over their fellows. Some of their number longed for ecclesiastical pre-eminence and preached accordingly. They wanted the ancient equivalent of election to the episcopacy or appointment to a large city church. They conformed their program to a pattern which seemed likely to secure this result.

With such an ultimate goal, the preacher would set up immediate goals for his preaching which would center around the desire to please and impress the right persons. After all, on one occasion in Israel's history only one prophet could be found, and he had to be brought from another locality for the purpose, who was sufficiently detached from motives of self-interest to say No to the king of Israel. It is significant that the other prophets, who numbered in the hundreds, are anonymous in the biblical account, while this one man has a name—Micaiah (I Kings 22:12-18).

With the exception of the prophets of the Baal cult, the Bible does not relate how the "false" prophets came to be included under this description. It may be that some of them began their prophetic careers as did the great prophets, in the first flush of enthusiasm and full dedication to their calling. The attrition of contemporary culture and the lust for power slowly dissipated this zeal. Perhaps unconsciously, they slipped over into the company of the prophets who had lost God and who still went through the motions of prophesying. Thus the true purpose of the prophet was corrupted and finally destroyed because he lacked inner resources to resist his world and his people.

The prophet Micah puts it bluntly and crudely: Cruel and unjust, insensitive to human need, using economic and political power brutally, the people applaud the man who pretends to be a prophet of God but who actually reflects their own moods and passions. Such a "prophet," Micah says, drunkenly hiccoughs his way through a sermon, which is ironically described by the incensed prophetic writer as devoted to praising the merits of some ancient equivalent of Four Roses or other alcoholic concoction (2:11). This irony reveals Micah's profound contempt for his contemporaries who succumb to popular demand and who preach pleasant words when furious words of condemnation are desperately needed. The pseudo prophets become furious, he adds in effect, only when their pay checks fail to come regularly from the church treasurer or are made out in amounts which are deemed too small.

When greed and spineless acquiescence in evil take away the prophet's passion for God's Word, the loss of his soul is not the only loss—revelation and vision perish, and spiritual darkness covers the land. The "prophets divine [preach] for money." (Mic. 3:11.) Micah's burning, angry words may well penetrate the conscience of all prophets, as they honestly search their hearts and struggle to keep their high calling undefiled by the corruption of the world in which they carry on their ministry.

The solution of the problem which faces all prophets when their first eagerness to be God's men begins to wane is presented by Jeremiah in his discussion of this problem in his own day. When Jeremiah contemplated the degradation of the prophetic leaders in a time of great national need, he cried out that his heart was broken (23:9). Both prophet and priest had turned from the true God and had devoted themselves to serving the people's whims and desires. They upheld evil practices, supported wickedness and sensuality, and perpetuated "ungodliness" in the land. And what is the reason for this shameful betrayal of their prophetic calling? The reply is put in the form of a question, to which each minister and prophet may give heed to his great profit:

For who among them [the false prophets] has stood in the council
   of the Lord
   to perceive and to hear his word,
   or who has given heed to his word and listened? (23:18).

The true prophet finds time to stand in the council of the Lord. When he does this, he hears God's word of salvation for his people and also for himself as he fights to keep his calling undefiled. This is the only way he can hold fast to his true purpose in life. What is the true purpose of the faithful prophet?

One way of getting at this question is to examine the various statements in the prophets' own accounts of their call. The prophet Isaiah provides us with significant information about his call. The word of the Lord asks: "Whom shall I send, and who will go for us?" After Isaiah responded, the Lord further declared: "Go, and say to this people . . ." (6:8, 9). The prophet's purpose, if he accepted the commission, was to go for God and on his behalf to speak to the people of his nation. Thus he was to be a spokesman bearing the Word of his God to Israel. The content of this Word will receive attention later in this study.

Jeremiah (ch. 1) reveals even more about the purpose of the prophetic ministry. He was told that God had appointed him to be a prophet to the nations of his day. He was to be sent and he would be told what he was to say. He would be set over nations and kingdoms in order "to destroy" and "to build."

And he would receive power to carry out his mission with firmness and courage. As in the case of Isaiah, he too was to "go and proclaim" the words which God imparted to him (2:2) in the hearing of the people of the community (Jerusalem).

The awesome and overwhelming vision which came to Ezekiel also contains suggestions as to the major purpose of the true prophet. In the first chapter we read such words as these: "The word of the Lord came to Ezekiel," "and when I saw it [the glory of the Lord], I fell upon my face." Chapter 2 is especially revealing: After the Spirit entered the prophet, he was commanded to stand up because God wanted to speak to him. Then he was told that he would be sent to the people of Israel that he might speak to them in words which God would give him. He was to speak these words, whether they heard or refused to hear. In a vision he ate a scroll which contained written words, presumably those the prophet was to speak. His function clearly was to pronounce the divine words regardless of the response which the people made to them. In Ezek. 3:18 the prophet's function is said to be that of warning the wicked so that death may not overtake them in their sin.

Space does not permit further presentation of material from the prophetic books, but the meaning of the evidence gathered is clear enough. The main aim of the prophet is to be God's spokesman. He is to be the man who is unequivocally devoted to the utterance of the divine Word, largely of judgment, to the people of the prophet's community. This Word must be spoken lest he be untrue to his call and his people perish in their persistent rebellion. The Word comes from God, is communicated through God's prophet, and is essential to the salvation of men. In this sequence the prophet is an important means of redemption, even though the Bible does not ignore other means whereby men may become aware of God's plan of deliverance. So to be fully, courageously, confidently, and devoutly the man who speaks for God is the great purpose of the prophet.

The words spoken by the prophet are words which represent the meaning of the peculiar history of the prophet's people Israel. And they are to be delivered to this people in order to remind them of what God has done for their salvation in the past and can do again and again in the present and future. Inasmuch as God's Word is directed to a people which has a special historical destiny involving other nations, this Word is also directed toward them at times, sometimes explicitly, but usually only implicitly.

As may readily be discovered by observing the nature of the prophet's program, the task and purpose of proclaiming the Word is not simply a matter of public speaking nor is the prophet's message a tape recording of what God had dictated to him previously. The Word is uttered, it is true; but its utterance depends upon its appropriation by the prophet as a person involved in the life of men and in the situation of sin which characterizes all mankind, beginning with the people of the community of faith.

More specifically, the prophet must serve as a watchman over the house of Israel. He must be on the lookout for evidence of wickedness, disobedience, and disloyalty to her Lord. These evils, if undetected and unchecked, would destroy God's community which he had chosen in order to demonstrate his love to men. In his capacity as watchman the prophet was obligated to watch events, social trends, national policies, international conflicts, with sharp eyes. His purpose was not to report them to his contemporaries in some kind of news weekly but to evaluate them boldly in terms of God's purpose of redeeming his people. This evaluation, however, would be derived from an extraordinary sensitivity of the prophet's spirit and mind. It would demand likewise of the prophet a unique realization of the work of Israel's God in history as transmitted through tradition and made known more directly through personal communion and worship. Its effect would always be envisioned in relation to God's ultimate purpose for Israel; never could it be viewed solely in relation to immediate events and problems.

The prophet was so conditioned by his background and call that he was enabled to extricate himself from the entanglements of his cultural situation long enough to detect their significance for God's redemptive plan. This temporary detachment enabled him to state this significance in vigorous and frequently denunciatory terms. Thus he warned the wicked for their wickedness and unrighteous deeds which were evidently performed largely in the context of individual life. He also warned the wicked nation of the consequences which would follow its faithless conduct.

How the latter type of warning was delivered, and the difficulty the prophet had in carrying out his mission, may be seen in the case of Habakkuk. This not-so-well-known prophet protested the burden that he was required to carry. Why did God keep pointing out to him the vastness of the wickedness, trouble, and violence which prevailed in the world and take no action to destroy it? For example, the dreaded Chaldeans were on the march (accepting the traditional view of this prophetic book) and war was at hand. Why did God permit this cruel nation to win victories and even to overthrow his own people Israel? On his watchtower, where the prophet is required to stand, at least psychologically, he saw the course of events in world history. From this perspective and with this function Habakkuk, and all true prophets, can understand and declare the true meaning of history. Then Habakkuk received a reply to his original question. The righteous man—or nation—lives by faith. This is the lesson that the watchman learns in a time of crisis. The true prophet can carry out his mission and fulfill his purpose by looking at history with the eyes of faith. Faith can be renewed and empowered by contact with the Lord of life in the creative silences of moments of meditation, even while he watches from his tower or in his study.

As an alert observer with special equipment the prophet can identify danger when it threatens without confusing the several kinds of danger which arouse the fears of men. Although he is not blind to the possibility of conquest by a military foe of Israel, the prophet is keenly aware that the real foe is within the nation. He recognizes the foe that subverts and erodes her faith and breaks down her integrity as a doer of justice and a lover of mercy for all of her people.

The true watchman of God is quick to detect the easy transfer of guilt for the evils of injustice and inhumanity to an external and easily identified foe, such as a foreign community or nation. Such ready rationalization is exposed as the sham that it is, and the real nature of the evil which exists is pressed home uncomfortably and persistently. The source of the difficulty is not the Chaldeans, the Egyptians, or the Edomites, the prophet insists. It is the unfaith and the idolatry of Israel herself.

What this means for the modern prophet when he fulfills the role of a prophetic watchman today is only too clear. Rejection and even vilification may be his lot. His identification of injustice in human relations in the name of the God of the Bible, when it becomes too specific, may be met by the accusation of unpatriotic subversion or even of affiliation with Communism. But the prophet as watchman is equipped with the knowledge of God and of his revealed demands to men. He does not employ standards which spell out the meaning of human community in language which is not God's. What he sees may be the breakdown of a nation's character or the substitution for integrity of glorified self-interest. To him this is a greater danger than an enemy's jet planes or ideological infiltration. Whether the latter exists or not, the former demands the attention of the prophet because it signifies an outright violation of the will of God. The possibility that the nation's return to the path of obedience may ward off national disaster is by no means the primary consideration. The fact that justice is the will of God, not that it may defend the "free world" from Communism, is the only religiously defensible reason for practicing it. The faithful watchman knows why he is watching and the effect of his watching also. He serves God by pointing out the presence of his people's sin and makes it possible for repentance and restoration to come if men give heed to his word.

The prophet preaches God's Word in respect to current history and recurring crises. This is his task and purpose. But he preaches this message for the sake of redemption, which has a far deeper and wider meaning than the preservation of the life and cherished institutions of any nation, even his own. Redemption relates to the universal human problem of man's relation to God, although it includes the host of subordinate problems which plague human beings.

It is not enough for the prophet to be on the alert for danger signals and to publish these when they become known. He must indicate their meaning for the collective and individual life of man, and their bearing upon the transhistorical purposes of God for his creatures. It is his obligation so to pronounce the meaning of events and practices as to exhibit before his listeners the divine work of redemption that is going on. Through his preaching, therefore, he communicates the possibility and method of repentance.

Sin is identified but the grace of God is magnified by the

stirring words of the prophetic preacher. The very language the prophet uses when preaching bears the full gospel directly or by implication even when the words are those of dreadful doom. The prophet's "The day of the Lord is at hand" is accompanied by "Seek the Lord and live."

The prophet confronts each man with the inescapable demand of the eternal God. In so doing he presents the relation of specific situations in the life of his people to the final situation in which man is called upon to make a fateful reply to his Redeemer. So that deliverance may come from this confrontation of each man by God in a crisis encounter, the prophet announces the divine demand for repentance and faith. This may appear in the form of an address to the nation, but it also points directly to each member of the community. The prophet tries to make available to his listeners the procedures and resources by which man may relate himself redemptively to his divine Savior. The result of this prophetic purpose is the communication of power instead of the impartation of truth.

The very word the prophet used, according to popular understanding in the biblical period, possessed a peculiar potency. It had an existence of its own and remained powerful even after the sounds which had voiced it had long since died away. The prophetic word was sent on its way by God, who provided for its reception and redemptive efficacy in the hearts of listeners. It accomplished this result without overriding the free will of any man. And when this Word finally became flesh, how effective it proved to be in searching the hearts of men, arousing slumbering consciences, and inspiring a triumphant faith! But before the time of Christ the incarnation of the Word in the life of the faithful prophet was evident when we see the response of Israel to his message. His words were not mere preachments;

they were expressions on the lips of the prophet of the cleansing, restoring power of God which possessed him.

In confronting each man with the Word of God's deliverance, the prophet was therefore more than a speaker; he was one who represented, indeed re-presented, the great work of salvation which the God of Israel had done for the fathers. God had presented this work in times past; the prophet was called to re-present it in his own day, that men might give heed and be saved.

In the light of this view of the prophetic purpose and function, the objection of such a prophet as Jeremiah to accepting the role was much more than the shyness of a young man diffident about making unpleasant public speeches. He did demur that he was too young to accept the office, but his principal objection may be stated in connection with the divine demand that the prophet exemplify, represent, God's work of redemption before his people. When he spoke and behaved as a prophet, men would be able to see in him the reality of repentance, forgiveness of sin, faithful obedience. The painful cries that were wrung from the lips of Jeremiah on more than one occasion and from those of Isaiah at least once reveal that spiritual travail and regeneration characterized these men who became prophets of God. One may see in at least some of their addresses the fact of their profound personal participation in the drama of deliverance which they were reporting to their hearers. The seriousness, the poignancy, of their speeches are indications of this participation, it appears to me.

Such a purpose as this, when considered in relation to contemporary preaching, is vastly illuminating especially for evaluating preaching on the basis of the prophetic standard in the Bible. It reveals the folly of superficial sermon preparation and of the slavish use of so-called sermon helps. There can be no question of sincerity or reality in preaching when the words that are uttered are confessions of sin and faith as well as sacramental representations of the presence of the living God. The prophet who utters these words is a man gripped by the power of God and stirred to the depths with gratitude for his own deliverance from sin. In the presence of his congregation the spokesman of God exemplifies and testifies to what God in his mercy has done for him, using the language of the community's faith and relating his words to their deepest needs.

Characteristically, the sermons that the prophets preach are completely devoid of maudlin sentimentality or tear-jerking phrases. Pitched on the sublime level of the will of the holy God whose glory fills the whole earth and whose mercy is beyond human utterance, their addresses have the splendor and majesty of the eternal hills or of the thunderstorm whose dark clouds are pierced by the flashing lightning. Because of their tremendous earnestness their words are deeply emotional, of course, and they stir the heart as well as the conscience. This impression, which the reader of their recorded words readily gathers, may be due partly to the occasional and spontaneous nature of their sermons. The prophets of Israel differ from the minister of a church in that they had no weekly task of sermon preparation. Nonetheless, the basic reason for their effective demonstration of the power of God within them was their conception of their task as witnesses to God's great deeds of salvation worked in them and available for all who heard and believed.

The preaching of the prophetic Word was sacramental in nature, just as it was also an act of the intellect and of ethical conviction on the part of the speaker. By the term "sacramental" is meant in this context the visible and audible presentation of the holy, righteous God to the assembly of the faithful. The Word which is spoken is the outer and audible symbol of this presence. It is an integral part of the total service of worship, contributing in a unique way to this experience, along with other sacraments, music, prayer, and the reading of Scripture. Among these it must be central if it is to be truly prophetic. For the Word that is spoken identifies and realizes the power, purpose, and action of God in a way that no other phase of worship can possibly do.

As it is central in Scripture, so it must be central in modern worship. In view of this function of preaching, the problem of the conflict between liturgical and nonliturgical services loses some of its weight. The living God cannot be worshiped apart from the worshipers' awareness of his merciful deeds, culminating in the deed of Christ. The nature and significance of these deeds requires recital, not only in chant and litany, but through the lips of a man of God to whom, as in the days of old, knowledge of these redemptive deeds has come with such compelling force that he is required to speak and to testify. The liturgy of the church must center around the memory and interpretation of these deeds. These deeds must be dramatized and appropriated by the worshiper through the use of every liturgical device at the church's disposal. The preacher and the altar can never be separated.

Not only must the prophet speak for God out of his knowledge and personal experience so that his words become the means of understanding and of worship. He must also so speak as to teach. His teaching function is not easily distinguished from his preaching task, although a distinction may be made. It is a part of his ministry because of the peculiar nature of his gospel, as shown in our discussion of his perspective. The substance of this gospel is the series of events which occurred crucially in Israel's history and which were instigated for his purposes by Israel's God. These had become the foundation of her faith. It was therefore imperative that they be remembered perpetually and that their bearing upon Israel's changing history be understood. Since these events, in particular the event of the covenant, were in the past, the people must be reminded of them regularly. The prophets, committed to speak the Word of the covenant God, were involved in the task of teaching this salvation-history and of explicating the ways in which it was related to their own day.

The frequency with which they refer to the covenant and to the release from Egypt which was theologically associated with it as the free act of divine grace illustrates this prophetic concern to teach the "essentials" of Israel's historical faith. Through their efforts these were not allowed to assume the status of tradition merely. The prophets related them so realistically and vigorously to the needs of the community that they effectually demonstrated the presence of the living God in the ongoing life of the people.

This is the reason for the importance of the prophets' teaching ministry. It kept alive the essential Word of God's salvation. Their teaching function, however, was not limited to the reiteration of the crucial events bearing on Israel's relation to her God. It included also the enunciation of principles based upon these events and upon the nature of the God who had instigated them for the guidance of the people in all their relationships and activities.

In this way the prophets were teachers of morality and of an ethical religion. They affirmed again and again, and in a variety of ways, the mandatory nature of righteousness. With the picturesque and concrete language of poetry they commanded the people:

Let justice roll down like waters,
and righteousness like an everflowing stream (Amos 5:24).

Lest there be any uncertainty as to the application of this principle, the prophets made their point explicit. In the court, in the market, in the sanctuary, and in the seat of government this injunction must be carried out. In this way all human relations would be purified by the power of the righteous God of the covenant community.

Such prophetic teaching is carried on in connection with the prophetic proclamation of the divine Word, of course. Apart from this, specific ethical instruction is inconceivable, for the prophetic mind knows no ethics as such. It comprehends only the concretely revealed reality of the living God who enters the human situation for the purpose of redeeming it and the men who are involved in it. This relation of ethics to theology must govern the modern preacher's view of his task also. He is required to face his congregation with stern ethical demands as he contemplates the kinds of evil which they do or in which they are acquiescent. His should be an instructive as well as an indignant response to the ethical questions that arise. Notwithstanding this, it is completely irrelevant for him to deal with moral issues *as such*. Detached from their framework within the gospel of divine love and justice, they become either reasonable lectures on morality or senseless scoldings which have no fundamental Christian or biblical meaning.

On the other hand, the prophet today finds it impossible to preach on theological themes which he submits to his congregation only as statements of truth which ought to be believed. His gospel knows no such statements of truth requiring only intellectual acceptance. The prophetic creed is indeed useful to denote the great truths of faith. But these truths symbolize the regenerating, life-giving power of the merciful God. He seeks to enter human life and demands absolute loyalty to his will in all that men think and do. Such a creed becomes a summons to action and to a world-transforming faith which possesses a radical moral power. So we must speak of prophetic ethics as theological ethics, provided we understand the peculiar biblical nature of theology. The prophet must conceive as inseparable his tasks of proclaiming the gospel and of enunciating its paramount ethical requirements.

We have seen that the great purpose of the prophet is to function as a man of God, his spokesman, dedicated completely to the work of making known the Word of salvation to his people. This Word which he must communicate is a Word of judgment and redemption, a Word of righteousness and compassion. It is also a sacramental Word whereby the very presence of the Savior-God may be realized. The prophet is a speaker, a teacher, and a representative of the God of Israel, who in the fullness of time appeared in Jesus Christ.

With this background of an understanding of the great purpose and task of the prophet, we may now investigate the biblical evidence as to secondary and derived purposes which moved the prophet to act in specific situations. These deal not only with public addresses, but with other kinds of action as well, the nature of which was determined by the situations he faced. As to specific preaching situations their occasions and the related prophetic objectives in preaching are many and varied. A cursory survey of the prophetic books will demonstrate this.

Secondary and immediate purposes to be found in the Bible relate to social and political crises or events which arouse the interest of the prophet. For example, war and revolution concern the prophets Ahijah and Elijah (I Kings 11, 18). In the first instance the intolerable tyranny of Solomon, who had exploited his people cruelly by using forced labor and imposing heavy taxes, was too much for his subjects and for some of the prophets. One of these waylaid a likely candidate for leadership over the northern tribes and dramatically and symbolically informed him of God's purpose to make him king of Israel. The task of Ahijah was to take direct political action at a critical period in the history of his people. He acted as a prophet in that he acted for God (11:31). He led a revolt against the house of Solomon, not because of Solomon's political failure, but because this ruler had turned to other gods. (The record reveals that political tyranny was also a factor.)

Later on the corrupt reign of Ahab and Jezebel, his queen, inspired Elijah to act. The background of the queen's hostility to the prophets of Israel's God need not concern us here. We should simply note that Elijah tried to stimulate a revival of the traditional Israelite faith by opposing the Tyrian faith of the queen. Certainly such an attempt had strong political implications, as may be seen by reading the biblical story. The fact that Elijah departed in haste after an apparent victory over the prophets of Jezebel reveals the human weakness of the prophet rather than uncertainty as to the demands of his God. Although the chronology of Elijah's life is not clear, evidently he lived to preach and to take political-prophetic action again.

In the eighth century B.C. the prophet Hosea became disturbed because of the political vacillation of the kings of Israel. They had been following a foreign policy which lacked integrity, consistency, and confidence in the power of Israel's God. He said the nation had acted like a silly dove, turning for an alliance first to Egypt and then to Assyria. This vacillation was accompanied by religious infidelity (the worship of the Baals) and by social corruption. Known chiefly for the strangeness of his marriage to the prostitute Gomer, Hosea was truly a prophet to his people. He lashed out at contradictions in national policy and at the nation's infidelity. The record does not state that he held personal conferences with Israel's state department. It does show that he spoke bluntly about its shortcomings, primarily for the purpose of exposing its lack of faith in the living God of Israel. This is the immediate purpose of the prophet's "political" action.

Characteristic of many speeches by Amos, Micah, Isaiah, and Jeremiah is the purpose of condemning specific forms of social evil. An attack upon those who oppress the small farmer is a case in point. Likewise sensuality, partly because of its ethical consequences, is satirically denounced. Woes are pronounced upon those who drink wine from huge bowls (Amos 6:6) and upon the man who with his son goes in to the same religious prostitute. This is denounced for moral and also for theological reasons.

Another aim of some sermons is the exposure of luxurious living. This is related closely to similar aims already named. Wealthy women who caused their men to crush the needy so that they could continue to eat and drink gluttonously were targets for the prophets' barbed words. Hypocritical devotion to the place and the forms of organized religion, especially the Temple and its cult, but also the local shrines, received its share of harsh denunciation also (Jer. 7; Amos 4:4-5; Isa. 1:12-17).

The purpose of such attacks was not the repudiation of worship in the sanctuary. Without doubt the purpose was the prophet's passionate desire to purify the cult and to make it serve the will of the altogether righteous God. The strong moral demands of this God were intimately involved in every act of worship directed toward him or offered in his name. If, as scholars are coming to believe increasingly, the prophet is associated with rather than detached from the cult, this concern of the great prophets for purity of worship in ethical terms becomes all the more understandable.

These examples of specific prophetic purposes are not complete, but they indicate the close connection between prophetic preaching and the life to which it is directed. One may observe significant omissions from these objectives when making comparisons with contemporary preaching. There is no appeal to support a program of ecclesiastical promotion, no campaign for financial contributions, no exhortations or lectures which present formulas whereby peace of mind and personal power may be gained, and no insistence upon belief in a particular formulation of a creed as indispensable to salvation.

These omissions may be explained in part by the fact that the prophets equated their congregations with the total national community, even though they singled out special groups for attention occasionally. They had no congregations in the modern sense of church membership. But there is an additional reason—their understanding that the gospel they preached dealt with the issues of life and death which confront all men and each man in the community of Israel. Their people were regarded as active, responsible, participating members of a community of faith and not primarily as citizens in a nation or a political order. The prophet's task was to be a promoter of the welfare of this community, a welfare that was defined by the God of the covenant. His work of promotion demanded evocation of faith and devotion to God as the only way to continue the community's true existence. Thus he must preach and teach, and in other ways as well impart to its members what that faith means.

The prophets' conception of their task and preaching purpose may be of great assistance to the modern preacher. He too struggles to adjust his professional objectives to the demands of the church as a social institution and as a community of believers. For him as for them there is the necessity of making all secondary purposes serve one major purpose. This purpose is to communicate to his people the Word which God has sent in Scripture and which he has implanted in the hearts of his prophets. By this means God uses him to deliver men from their sin. Such preaching relates them to one another in justice and love and to their Redeemer in faith and grateful obedience.

IV

The Prophetic Preacher's Power

THIS IS A POWER-WORSHIPING GENERATION. AND PREACHERS are power-seeking persons, corrupted by the lust for power which is typical of their age and toward which their human nature is inclined. Prone to attack manifestations of power in the machine, in politics, and in business, the preacher is peculiarly susceptible to its evil effects and peculiarly insensitive to his sin. He is especially vulnerable to the corrupting effects of power, for its possession is held to be proof of his success as a leader in church and community. He thrills to the acclaim of congregation and press when his pulpit oratory is said to represent "powerful" preaching. When personal appearance, tone, manner, and delivery make an impression upon the listeners in the pew, the preacher is bound to hear about it. He faces the temptation of evaluating his performance in harmony therewith.

The modern minister in the Protestant church is the personal center of attention. Everything revolves about him during the service, even though the pulpit may be set to one side in the chancel to conform to a liturgical conception of worship. There he stands in front of his people, noticed by all. And he speaks often with great assurance on the mightiest themes which have

64

occupied the attention of the human mind. His every tone, gesture, mannerism, are noted and remembered either to his credit or for future referral to the committee on pastoral relations. With words of commendation ringing in his ears after an unusually eloquent sermon, he is unavoidably affected by his "success" and develops habits which will maintain and increase his advantage over his less fortunate brothers. He may even adopt for use in private conversation or in addresses before the Rotary Club the professional manner used in his pulpit. Unless he has a corrective, he will increasingly cultivate this kind of power in his ministry. In all this unfortunate development, he profoundly misses the meaning of his calling as a prophet and the real nature of prophetic power.

There should be no misunderstanding at this point. The power of the preacher-prophet to win and hold attention is important, as is his ability to influence people through the art of speech. What he may legitimately do with voice, argument, and persuasive address to secure this result, he must do. But we are not dealing here with these matters, but rather with the nature of real power whereby a congregation not only listens attentively but hears and receives the actual Word of the prophet's God. Conceivably, and it has happened, a thin, piping voice, an unimposing appearance, and a simple sermon totally lacking in the refinements of logic and theology may manifest genuine prophetic power. Hearing and receiving the Word of the revealed gospel is the test of authentic prophetic power. Not popular approval, professional advancement to larger churches or positions of administrative responsibility in the church, but success in accomplishing the one task which the prophet is called to do—the effective communication of God's Word—this is convincing proof that he has received power from on high. In the possession of this power he is protected against accepting the illusion of power which comes from the plaudits of men.

Power of any sort represents the ability to get certain results. These results are measured in terms of the goals which are reasonably identified with any given activity or expenditure of energy. The power of the atomic bomb is measured by the extent of the devastation it can produce in buildings and to life upon the earth. This can be determined by observation with instruments and by examination with the human eye. There is the power of public opinion which can be so controlled as to destroy a reputation, produce a war, elect a candidate for public office, or sell a particular brand of whiskey.

There is also the power of knowledge which enables man to exploit natural resources and to improve the physical conditions of his existence. And there is the power of sheer goodness, whereby unselfish love, sacrifice beyond the call of duty, and imaginative concern for others achieves positive results. Power is the capacity to secure those results which are envisioned by those who use it, whether it relates to physical energy, social relations, or is of the human spirit. It is important to distinguish carefully between the various kinds of power with which men deal.

The power of the true prophet has a distinctive character which must be the chief concern of the preacher if he is not to lose his soul in false service to his Lord. The power of persuasive speech, of personality, of community leadership, of skill in human relations, of intelligence, of public opinion, and of propaganda for the cause of the gospel must not be minimized by him. But these must all be subordinated to the greatest power of all—that which God provides to those whom he calls to be his true ministers. We do not know very much about these lesser forms of power in the experience of Israel's prophets. As to the power of speech, for example, there are no recordings of the prophet's voice, as there may be, incidentally, in centuries to come of the voices of great preachers now living. No ancient Hebrew editor produced an "I Can Hear It Now" recording, so that the very tones and accents of Hosea and his eighth-century contemporaries can come to our ears.

That these men had the power of effective speech is undeniable. They drew and held crowds; they got reactions, sometimes unpleasant. They were not easily forgotten, although much that they said the people wanted to forget. Late in the seventh century defenders of the genuineness of Jeremiah's prophetic calling found it possible to recall and quote the words of Micah, who lived one hundred years earlier:

Zion shall be plowed as a field;
Jerusalem shall become a heap of ruins (Jer. 26:18; Mic. 3:12).

These were indeed memorable words, for could not the tourist from Judah still visit the ruins of the northern kingdom and learn their lesson of coming doom? Could not the Hebrews read how Hezekiah of Judah had heeded Micah's words and thus warded off the downfall of his kingdom? Micah had preached with power in the name of the God of judgment. The king spared his life because he spoke authoritatively.

The power which was so effectively exercised by the Hebrew prophets may be described in several ways. We may speak of their intellectual use of this power, for example. Theirs was not primarily a ministry to the mind, nor was theirs a power especially characterized by its intellectual quality. Its uniqueness lay in another realm, as will be noted later. Notwithstanding this fact, the prophets possessed a keen discernment, a penetrating intelligence, which is often overlooked by the modern student. Their acuteness of mind was highly impressive. They were quick to analyze a problem and to identify its crucial elements with great precision. Perhaps they were so successful in their brilliant diagnoses of the illnesses of their times because they were fundamentally simple men unacquainted with the intricacies of abstruse logic or metaphysical speculation. In the language of the psychologist William James, they were "tough-minded" rather than "tender-minded" thinkers, looking at the world of experience as the real theater of divine action.

For this reason every social situation, every national event, every conflict with which they were concerned, was critically appraised. This they did with an incisiveness and searching scrutiny which has hardly any parallel in the history of human thought. When they spoke, they did so with a deep understanding and with clear utterance. Their intellectual authority would have been perfectly obvious had it not been for the fact that it was overshadowed by the religious orientation of their speeches and writings.

One reason for their success in this area was their complete objectivity. This is the objectivity not of the scientist but of the man of faith who sees all experience ultimately in the perspective of an Other who confronts him in his world. Through this encounter with God the prophet gained an understanding of all experience and all truth. He could not commit the fallacy of confusing his own ideas and hopes with those which were supported by universal reality. The prophet Ezekiel spoke of the folly of those who did this and made the mistake of identifying their own visions with ultimate truth (13:3). Those who did this were blind to the real truth. They were unable to assess the situation in which the nation found itself in a time of crisis. They were wise men but not wise with the wisdom of God.

They proposed utterly inadequate defenses for the city. Using an architectural figure, the prophet says they daubed the flimsy walls (defenses) with whitewash. This gave them the appearance of solidity. They lent the authority of religion to defenses which were not religious. They sanctified military and economic measures but did not call for repentance for the nation's neglect of God. The true prophet identified those who "set up idols in their minds" (14:3 Amer. Trans.) and were unable to penetrate to the truth of the people's desperate spiritual plight. These he condemned in the hope that the nation would seek the God of the covenant and turn to him for salvation.

The way in which the true prophet lashed out at the "false" prophets suggests the power of his intelligence in its relation to his task. The men whom he placed in the category of "false" prophets, no matter what their virtues and social contribution, are described. He analyzed the sources of their power effectively. After doing this, the prophet Jeremiah concluded that they had no authority nor did their utterances ring true. They had failed to refer what they preached to the source of all truth for verification. They had cut themselves off from the God of truth and power. None of them had the courage to stand in the "council of the Lord, to see and hear his word" (Jer. 23:18 Amer. Trans.). By standing before him the genuine prophets received assurance that their words were compatible with his Word of salvation. This divine frame of reference authenticated what they preached so cogently to the day in which they lived. This is intelligence of a high order.

Here is a matter of significance for the preacher today. From the prophets he may learn that he may be profound and also simple, learned yet understandable, pious yet possessed of intellectual integrity. The ability to confuse by the vastness of one's erudition is not a necessary mark of learning. The power of the intellect can receive no better demonstration than the demonstration of such a successful discovery and formulation of the truth that it can be transmitted to the minds of others. We have seen that the prophets were impatient to the point of anger at the fancies and obscurities of pseudo-religious leaders who had no outer or compelling criterion for evaluating their ideas or no deep passion to express them in the simplest possible terms. Was the popular view of true prophecy in their time identified with the incoherence and unintelligibility of the sounds that issued from the mouths of the prophets? This is certainly a possibility.

On the other hand, we observe in connection with Moses, whom tradition viewed as a prophet, a contrasting point of view. God declares that he did not come to him or speak to him in dreams or visions—as he did to the prophets—but with face-to-face instructions:

> Mouth to mouth do I speak with him,
> Plainly, and not in riddles (Num. 12:8 Amer. Trans.).

With such instructions Moses, and the great prophets also, could speak clearly and convincingly to their people. Of interest is the relevant comment of Paul at a much later time: "In church I would rather speak five words with my mind, in order to instruct others, than ten thousand words in a tongue [which only God could understand]" (I Cor. 14:19). In intelligent simplicity and clarity which is derived from a personal knowledge of the gospel lies authority for the prophet.

This achievement must be credited to the prophets, although they are so constantly acclaimed today as social reformers that it is often unrecognized. That they did this so well suggests another principle which is useful in this evaluation of our own ministry by reference to the prophetic norm—intellectual clarity has a moral quality which is closely related to intellectual integrity. The prophet's understanding of the world from the standpoint of his vision of the God who called him, coupled with the incisive relevance of his presentation of this understanding, was more than a rational comprehension of reality. Upon these men rested a heavy obligation to know and to impart the Word of their God with all its ramifications for human existence. They came to this knowledge by no easy route, although God's coming to them was its beginning. Thought and toil, reflection and suffering, were the price they had to pay in their struggle to arrive at the meaning of the revealed Word which they were required to preach. This sense of obligation and the resulting strenuous effort to understand and to articulate the Word to their fellow countrymen faithfully and fully lent a moral quality to their effort which is not usually associated with intellectual reflection.

This reasoning indicates that the power of the prophet was also a moral power. The view that the prophets were men of unsurpassed moral strength correctly interprets their prophetic ministry. They cannot be called moral reformers, contrary to the general understanding of the true prophet's function and interest. Their principal purpose was neither social reconstruction nor moral regeneration for the individual. Yet the power which operated through them had a substantial influence in these areas and upon the lives of the prophets as individuals. They were dedicated to the proclamation of the supreme goodness of God, although they aimed at declaring more than this, as a later discussion of the prophet's proclamation will show. They were wholeheartedly committed to the preaching and implementation of the righteousness of God in the total life of the

Israelite community. This was the objective of their moral effort, dominating them as persons and also as professional preachers.

They gathered up and vividly affirmed the great ethical insights of their culture. For this reason their words had ethical relevance. The prophets appealed to the heart and conscience of their hearers when they preached words of condemnation and hope (Jer. 11:20). In this sense they were the proponents of an ethical doctrine and could speak to the conscience of the nation. As interpreters of a high morality they gave themselves to the task of unmasking duplicity and corruption in the social order. They denounced what and whom they ruthlessly exposed in the name of the Source of righteousness in the universe. They were driven by a strong moral indignation, which was supported by a revealed knowledge of God. They struck out at current immoralities with vigor and courage. They were thoroughly persuaded that the word of doom that they brought was not a prediction of disaster for opposing an impersonal moral order. It was instead the doom of divine judgment for flaunting the righteous will of God. The prophets' moral effectiveness is thus to be found in a true theological perspective—the existence and purpose of the covenant God of Israel. His ethic is a theological ethic. And his moral power exists because of that.

For their ethical principles these men depended upon the overarching reality which had manifested itself in the form of the redeeming, creating, judging God of their fathers. They had only one justification and support for their moral understanding—the righteousness residing in the heart of the Eternal. They knew that they could preach the good life only by preaching the demands made by life with him. It was not the impressiveness of their burning anger which constituted the power of these men. It was the extreme devotion and zeal they exhibited for the performance in the social process of the righteous will of the Lord of history.

In view of his revelation to them their knowledge of morality was largely intuitive and immediate. The influence upon them of Israel's traditions and history and of other factors which contribute to the moral education of the individual in any age must also be recognized. The divine sanction for their ethical judgments was regarded as paramount by the prophets and by the people whose lives they condemned. Their opponents seldom attacked the basic presuppositions of the prophets. These were accepted, even though their implications for daily life were often denied. Both prophets and people shared a theistic point of view, as was generally true of non-Israelite peoples as well.

What distinguished the prophets from their culture, however, was their refusal to accept the conscience of the group as truly representative of the goodness of God. They radically realized how often and how seriously its judgments and conduct patterns were in outright contradiction of those which were desired and commanded by Israel's God. Hence their power could not possibly derive from the moral force of the community. They were empowered by knowledge of a supreme ultimate morality which derived from the objective existence of the self-revealing God. This morality was different from, and indeed often in opposition to, the sum total of the ethical insights of society's moral leaders. Undoubtedly the preaching of the prophets conveyed a sense of this unique power to those who listened to them.

The peculiar power of which the prophets felt themselves to be instruments was in the last analysis neither intellectual, moral, nor personal. To learn what it really was, we may recall the inaugural experiences of the prophets and other narratives in the Bible which record their intimate encounters with God. The root of this common Semitic name for Deity connotes power. One of the two most frequently used names for God in the Old Testament has this root meaning and, interestingly enough, occurs in the plural form— Elohim, *El* being the basic root.

- Pre-eminently the God of the Bible was a powerful being; that is to say, he had the power to accomplish what he willed in terms of his total nature. So God's power was exerted as the expression in nature and in history of his dynamic, creative, redemptive relationship to the world. This power worked in and beyond nature, through and in spite of man, in fulfillment of the divine plan for God's creatures. It would ultimately overcome all obstacles but never denied to man the freedom which he received at his creation. This plan was made known to men in the Word, the disclosure of which is the sole purpose of the prophet's existence. The content of the Word came from the revelation of the Discloser of history's meaning. The prophet's power to make this Word known to men came also from the God who alone could make its communication effective.

, The term which most aptly expresses the support which God gave his prophets when they declared his will to men is spirit. In the biblical tradition this word affirms the life which God possesses and which he shares with men, not in the form of being, but in the form of power and function. By it men are energized, inspirited, empowered, in a remarkable way for the realization of the mission which is laid upon them. God's Spirit was poured out upon the prophet Micah. He was filled with power, the only kind of power which the prophet can use— the power against strong opposition and deep prejudice boldly to attack the sins of Israel. Spirit possession was demonstrated not by foaming at the mouth or ranting incoherently about religion. Its presence was proved by the courageous words of opposition to evil which God moved the prophet to pronounce. And its presence was also seen in the majestic and exalted form which his denunciations assumed. Far from being hackneyed or petty, the prophetic rebuke was raised to the lofty level of divine wrath voiced by the One whose holiness fills the whole earth.

When the Spirit of the Lord came upon the prophet, he became a new man, capable of seeing human sin in a new light and of addressing himself to it with undreamed-of effectiveness. The prophet thus received a reorientation toward the world in which he lived. On the basis of this he acted with a power which he had not previously had. This was what happened to Saul (I Sam. 10:6), to Jeremiah, Ezekiel, and to other prophets of the Old Testament. In a sixth-century prophetic book the writer states that this is how the prophets of Israel received their words from God: "The words which the Lord of hosts had sent *by his Spirit* [italics supplied], through the former prophets" (Zech. 7:12). An unusual story is told by the prophet Ezekiel (3:1-14) when he sets forth an account of his authority as a prophet. The prophet identifies the supernatural nature of his call in spite of the strange imagery of the first chapter. He then describes the amazing events by means of which he was equipped with power and with a message for his generation. In a vision a hand extends to him a scroll with writing upon it. He eats, not his own words, but the words of God inscribed thereon. Then, he says, "a spirit lifted me up and carried me away" (Amer. Trans.). Like Ezekiel, the true prophet is carried away by the Spirit of God. This doesn't mean that he loses control of the situation. He lets God take control and is thereby enabled to function with greater power and freedom.

The gift of the prophetic Spirit is an important part of the Bible's understanding of prophetic authority. One prophet's oracle includes words pertinent to this point which are ascribed to God: " 'Not by arms, nor by force, but by my spirit, says the Lord of hosts' " (Zech. 4:6b Amer. Trans.). This power of the Spirit is the power which is finally efficacious against the resources and power systems of men. A late postexilic prophecy which looks to the future for the complete vindication of God's people thinks of a time when the divine Spirit will come to all men in the redeemed community. When God pours out his Spirit, all men will become prophets. Here we see how important the conception of a Spirit-filled prophetic person had become in Israel's traditions. The new age will see the universalization of this experience in the entire membership of the community (Joel 2:28).

The prophetic Messiah (Isa. 11:2-5, 9) also shows the effect of this tradition. The Messiah will possess wisdom and understanding, counsel and might, knowledge and reverence. He will have judicial discernment, compassion for the needy, a mouth for severe condemnation, a character of righteousness and faithfulness. And he will be full of the spirit of the Lord. This chapter comes very close to a full description of the true prophet. And it states the effect of such prophecy—the earth will be filled with the knowledge of God as the waters cover the sea.

These illustrations point to the conclusion that to be filled with the Spirit of God was an experience that had a special meaning for the prophet of Israel. It meant the possession of the power sent by God for the faithful performance of the prophetic office. Other biblical examples of spirit-filled activity, such as frenzied dancing, speaking with tongues, and prostration, are largely repudiated and despised by the true prophets. The prophetic power which is associated with God's Spirit, while supernatural in nature and origin, cannot be mechanistically or irrationally conceived. It is power which unites with and transforms the capacities and powers of the human beings to whom it comes. It arouses in them latent capacities of dedication, understanding, and heroic action which were previously unknown.

The possibility of such a remarkable experience is predicated upon the biblical doctrine of man. He is a being made in the divine image and possessing God's Spirit. He can achieve his highest possibilities only by the life of faith and obedience to his creator. Apart from this doctrine the whole concept of the spirit of prophecy is meaningless. Using it as a fundamental premise, however, this concept is highly intelligible and meaningful. Man's created nature which includes the Spirit of God is obviously able to respond to the Creator. Man may receive whatever gifts God sees fit to bestow, even the special gift of the spirit of prophecy. This gift endues chosen persons with the power to understand and to declare to their generation the Word of their Creator and Redeemer. The problem of the relation of the spirit which man receives at creation to the prophetic Spirit did not concern the prophets. Both belong to biblical psychology, and both interacted to produce the prophet of God.

In any case, the prophets were sure that this gift had come to them, although they did not always try to explain the manner of its coming or its relation to their day-by-day moods and emotions. This certainly is seen in their lives, their resistance to pressure from rulers, leaders of the hierarchy, and their own families. Their courageous speeches and writings, the clarity and cogency of their thought, the depth and genuineness of their radicalism, show this too. Their course was not made easy through the presence of God's Spirit. It was, in fact, made more difficult. The rigorous demands of the God who was present were vastly more severe and urgent than those of a remote, traditional God could possibly be. The God at hand could not be escaped or disobeyed. How some of the prophets longed to get away from him!

> O that I had in the desert
> a . . . lodging place. (Jer. 9:2.)

But escape was impossible. His Spirit possessed them and would not let them go. The insistence and harshness of his demands increased their discomfort and also intensified the vigor with which they spoke. At the same time they deepened and further confirmed the prophet's belief that he was under bondage to carry out a divine mission regardless of the consequences.

He was no longer his own man—God owned him, and he would be unspeakably miserable if he preached not the divine word. One of these men was driven to such depths of despair and pain that he cried out:

> Cursed be the day
> on which I was born! (Jer. 20:14) .

But he never betrayed the trust that God had imposed in him. Boldly he made known the meaning of events according to the mind of God and was steadfast to the end. Controlled by God's Spirit, the prophets received a renewal of power and in their hearts a recurring reinforcement of their desire to serve the One who had sent them into the world to do his bidding.

The effect of this power upon the prophet's actual preaching is also evident. Here, if anywhere, is where the student of prophetic preaching would expect to discover the power of God. The prophet is speaker for God the Speaker and will surely speak so that the divine message to men may be heard and understood. His power was given to him for the sole purpose of making him an effective proclaimer of that message. It is a power which impresses the hearer with the intellectual · challenge, the moral appeal, and the divine authority of the words that are spoken. By this power the words are driven home into the mind, the conscience, the life, of man. By this power the words coming from the prophet's lips are transformed into the divine Word of judgment, mercy, and salvation. When it is fully present, the prophet with his religious heritage, his personality, and his official status in his community recedes into the background; and his audience sees and hears only God. The preacher becomes a witness and an instrument in the hands of his Redeemer.

In this transforming experience of true prophecy such is the wonder of the life of God within men, the very control of the prophet's consciousness by the Spirit of God serves to mobilize his capacities and talents in a remarkable way. He is likely to be at his very best when he has most completely yielded himself to God and subdued his natural impulses. His voice carries conviction; his tones are strong and clear; his face is alight with his eagerness and determination. His words are persuasive and pungent, and his thought realistically illuminates the mystery of man's life as he expounds the purpose of God for his people. The power that is within him lends to the prophetic sermon that relevance to man's religious situation, that note of authority for his listeners, and that penetrating personal meaning which signifies that it comes from God and must be obeyed. This power makes possible the response of faith, but it never causes the annihilation of man's will. When the Word is preached with this divine power, men may reject it or receive it; they can never be neutral with respect to it. God makes clear to them that there are only these two answers to his prophetic Word.

With the power which is his by the grace of God the prophetic preacher is supremely attentive to one objective—secondary purposes and aims are recognized as such. Selection of theme for the sermon, use of illustration, organization of material, and manner of delivery are controlled by his main aim. His passionate determination to proclaim the divine Word is united with the power which makes its proclamation possible. Such a preacher does not need to be told to preach first the kingdom of God. The Spirit of God which dwells in him witnesses to his spirit that the kingdom is the entire gospel. It embraces the complete meaning of the redeeming Word, and this he must preach lest he perish. Then his impulse to deal with secondary or even trivial themes is checked as sheer blasphemy. He will preach only the mighty Word of salvation as this is set forth in the biblical revelation. He will present this as the way of life and hope for men who are in desperate need. His discourse will be lifted to the plane of dignity and seriousness which is required by this purpose. He will try to be interesting although he will find that his Spirit-directed choice of themes will arouse its own interest, since it will deal with the deepest issues of life and death. Thus the power of the prophet which is not his yet peculiarly his own fixes his attention upon the primary meaning of salvation and effectively supports him in communicating it to others.

Of course there are difficulties which stand in the way of a preacher's use of this essential power. Some are peculiar to the mind-set and temper of our time, while others are common to all periods of history, including that of Israel's prophets. Others are, of course, peculiar to the culture of the period in which the prophets live. One of these difficulties is modern man's intense self-consciousness and self-reliance, even in those areas which are supposed to deal with faith in God. The preacher tacitly and also expressly admits the existence of God. He may even seek to realize the prophetic goal in his ministry.

In spite of this he may be intellectually incapable of experiencing the power which his biblical faith identifies and exalts because of the strains of naturalistic philosophy and humanistic ethics in his cultural development and his formal education. It may seem strange and even fantastic for him to imagine that he thinks the thoughts of Another, that his vital energies are quickened by a power not his own. He may think it incredible that the truth which burdens his soul was not developed by his unaided intelligence! Surely the training which he has so carefully secured, the talents which he has so diligently cultivated, and the professional skills which are applauded by his admirers are his own personal achievement. It hurts his pride and offends his intelligence to suppose that a Being upon whom he is utterly dependent is the only true source of preaching power.

On the other hand, the Hebrew prophet was equally proud and independent, although his was not a naturalistic philosophy which excluded the intervention of the supernatural. His desire for self-determination was qualified by his recognition of the impinging reality of the superhuman spiritual order. He readily accepted the possibility of the entrance into his life of an extraneous power claiming his complete obedience. He objected only when this possibility became a personal reality for himself. Perhaps the difference between the preacher of Israel and many of us can be phrased simply. The former readily accepted the possibility of faith. He acted on the basis of those attitudes that faith alone can engender. Today this is not always the case. A survey among American leaders entitled "This I Believe" turned out for one half of those queried to be belief in anything but God.

The truly effective preacher of our day is a man who has responded in faith to the living God of biblical faith. He has obtained power through that response to do the work of a prophet among men. In the absence of this faith the preacher ceases to exist. He has become a lecturer whose principal interest is the various phenomena of religion. And with the destruction of the preacher the church too disappears. The church is the divinely chosen community of forgiven sinners which cherishes the remembered acts of God for its deliverance. It seeks to make them known to those who are on the outside through faithful witnessing and preaching of the Word.

Obstacles to faith were and are obstacles to the possession and use of prophetic power for preaching. The true prophet knows full well that there is a divine order upon which the world of men and the forces of nature continuously and ultimately depend. When this power captures and commands him, he acts in obedience to it. Then he discovers that it is renewed within him and that it stands by him in his routine activities and in every crisis in his career as a prophet.

Faith is therefore the secret of its appropriation and its continued availability to the prophetic preacher. It alone enables him to possess the power of the true prophet. It alone permits him to be blessed by all the resources that he really needs to be a true spokesman of God. Through the power of God the weak prophet becomes strong. His word will be invincible and potent: "Is not my word [spoken on behalf of God by the prophet] like fire . . . and like a hammer which breaks

82

the rock in pieces?" (Jer. 23:29). It is delivered with smashing, crushing force, annihilating smugness, pride, sin, and the polite inattentiveness of some Sunday morning congregations. And it also is a healing Word, wooing men to God and showing them the power of his love. In behalf of such a God the modern Hosea may plead:

How can I give you up, O [my children]!
. . . .
    my compassion grows warm and tender (Hos. 11:8).

V

The Prophet's Perspective

THE PROPHET POSSESSED A CONSUMING PASSION TO BE GOD'S MAN
and spokesman. Available to him was an inexhaustible source
of power to proclaim the Word of redemption with intellectual
incisiveness, moral conviction, and divine authority. With this
equipment the prophetic preacher addressed his words and
program to his people in relation to the mind-set and culture
which characterized the period in which he lived. To be understood by them he had to clothe the divine Word of his message
in the particular words which had meaning for his own
generation.

In spite of his peculiar power and call he was a product of
his own day. So he was compelled to articulate the truth he
brought in the language of his contemporaries. He did this,
even though, as has been made clear, he often rejected patterns
of thought and action which were cherished by his people.
This posed a serious problem for the prophet, since he was
required to distinguish between the ways of God and the ways
of men if he was to succeed in establishing genuine communication.

For this reason the minister seeking to learn the biblical
lesson of effective prophetic preaching needs to learn what

the prophet's perspective was. He must realize how the prophet looked at the world in its physical, cultural, social, and religious aspects. He must observe the prophet's use of popular beliefs in communicating his own distinctive viewpoint. In this way today's preacher may identify the interests and insights which were peculiar to the biblical prophet's own day and those which have universal relevance and value.

The people of Israel were faced by the necessity of coming to terms not with just one way of life but with two. The nomadic ideal was confronted by the Canaanite. The latter was based on a long-established civilization which had tremendous prestige. An awareness of its power over their people is frequently indicated in the prophetic writings. The way in which it influenced the preaching of the prophets may be gathered by noting some of its salient features. These may be considered for the light they throw on the message of the prophets and for the frequent and striking parallels they present to aspects of our own culture.

Over against the tribal society whose patterns persisted for centuries in the life of Israel there was set the commercial-agrarian culture which was indigenous to Palestine and associated with a settled existence. This the Hebrews found already established in Palestine when they arrived there. City states, strongly fortified, were flourishing centers of trade from lands round about. Semiarid land was tilled by the occupants of villages, and its produce was brought to the larger trade centers to be disposed of in the markets there. Owners of land tended to increase their holdings and to move to the city, thus becoming absentee landlords. They ruthlessly foreclosed mortgages (Mic. 2:2) and became members of the nonproducing class in the large cities. In this fashion the small landowner slowly disappeared and with him the middle class which could have served as a buffer between the wealthy and the very poor. The latter thus became more numerous. The result was inevitable—extremes of prosperity and poverty in society. It is well to notice that this situation received considerable attention from the prophets, as a casual reading of Amos, Micah, Isaiah, will show.

The prophet was not a champion of the so-called proletariat. however. Although caught in the middle of acute tensions created by this situation, the prophet ardently proclaimed the need for justice for the sake of the God of Israel. The covenant of this God had stipulated kindness toward all members of the community. The prophet did not betray his calling by yielding to the temptation to become a social reformer. He was always the spokesman whose word of repentance and redemption included but was never superseded by the word of social justice which needed to be spoken.

It is obvious that present tensions in the social-economic order offer temptations to the preacher which may readily be compared with those faced by the men of Israel. I need merely mention the conflict between agriculture and industry, or more properly, between an agricultural and an industrial economy, to reveal one important phase of the social unrest which the Christian minister must face if he is to fulfill his function as a prophetic preacher. Should he take sides when the moral issues are clearly drawn, as seems sometimes to be the case? If he does, will his partisanship jeopardize his effectiveness as a minister? The prophet of Israel provides the answer to the problem posed here, as he does for so many other baffling questions which harass the preacher of today—the preacher speaks for God, who demands radical repentance of all men, owner and worker, employer and employee, rich and poor, as well as justice between them.

Tied up to the unstable and insecure economy of Israel was a resplendent and impressively sensuous religion. This religion reflected a conception of reality which sharply opposed that preached by the prophets. Viewed superficially, the practice of this religion was eye-catching and thrilling indeed. Its magnificent pageantry consisted of religious processions wherein the images of richly adorned gods and goddesses were carried (Isa. 46:1) on the occasion of a festival or national crisis. It involved elaborate ceremonies on various occasions in the agricultural year.

The chief function of the god and goddess (Baal and Asherah) was to promote the fertility of the soil, the herd, and the human family. Consequently the method of "worship" was largely the practice of imitative magic. The desired action of the divine couple was secured through the performance by the worshipers of the act of sexual intercourse at the shrine. This was supposed to stimulate the god and goddess to do their part with resulting fertility and prosperity. Associated with the shrine were sacred prostitutes whose duty it was to permit the use of their bodies by the male worshipers. Hosea is thought to have married a prostitute (priestess) of some Palestinian shrine, perhaps that in his home village. There were male prostitutes also, the records reveal (II Kings 23:7). In connection with this Canaanite-Israelite fertility cult not only offerings of chastity were made but also those of the fruit of the field, the flock, and the womb. The practice of human sacrifice undoubtedly occurred, although there is no evidence that it was common among the Israelites (I Kings 16:34; Mic. 6:7).

The cult I have tried to describe, however briefly, was understandably popular in Israel, even though it was Canaanite in origin rather than Israelite. Its sensuous appeal, its promise of prosperity, and its association with the sophisticated life of the Canaanites proved to be irresistible to the Hebrew people. So it was a serious obstacle to the success of the prophets, whose gospel stood for dedication to the righteous God of Israel and faithful obedience to his will. Baalism was more than a religion to be observed with the eye and enjoyed sensuously by men. It was a kind of philosophy, a view of ultimate reality. It is this underlying character of the religion of Canaan which made it such a threat to the faith that the prophets preached.

Mechanistic Baalism was by definition impersonal. Relations between its gods and the worshipers were impersonal, involving sensory stimuli, magical coercion, and ritualistic control. The personal values of love, forgiveness, faith, obedience, so important in prophetic preaching, were absent from Baalism. The gods were devoid of real moral purpose or power. They failed consistently to speak a word of condemnation or rebuke to the human situation when such a word was greatly needed. Thus they were tacitly in favor of the schemes of men for the exploitation of their fellows, since even in the abode of the gods silence meant consent.

The sensuous, materialistic, impersonal faith of the Palestinian was bound to leave unchecked the social trends toward extreme wealth and extreme poverty, toward the disruption of the land economy, toward the excessive enjoyment of food and drink, and toward national disintegration. As we shall see in a later chapter, the only group that sought to stem the tide of ruinous corruption was the prophets. These did raise their voices in the name of their God with vigor and courage in times of national crisis induced by external foes and internal evil. In so doing, they revealed that the Baalism of their day had not been without effect upon their minds. The nature of this influence will more appropriately be included in the discussion of the prophet's theological perspective, to which we shall turn shortly.

Without question Canaanite culture and thought affected the prophets both positively and negatively. It was the prevailing way of looking at life in their time. It had to be reckoned with, just as the modern minister must react to the secular view of life which opposes the faith he preaches. Ways in which the secularism of our time resembles the Baalism of the prophets' day are readily detected. The cult of sex in our time is one. It is true that its practice and ritual are usually not found in the church. Yet the cult persists. How colorful is the action which its devotees take to adore the female body beautiful! Press notices, enormous displays in front of theaters, and gorgeous forms on the color screen all indicate that there are only unimportant differences between the ancient Asherah and the modern Marilyn Monroe. This cult conditions the minds and hearts of his listeners probably more than the modern preacher knows or cares to know. It must affect his preaching to them in a vital way, as it did the prophets of old.

Baalism, using the words and forms of religion, relied upon the primacy of things and material goods, the abundance of which was a measure of successful living. The gods were conveniences for accomplishing this end, whether their worshipers actually understood this aspect of their nature or not. For the Baal-loving Israelites the real kingdom of God was a kingdom of goods, economic power, sated appetite, and control of others as means to these ends. Food, wine, winter and summer houses, sex, land, prestige, were desirable possessions which the cult fully approved and even openly encouraged.

The prophets faced the extremely difficult task of preserving the Israelite faith in its essential aspects while accepting the good that Baalism clearly afforded. But they had to do this by accommodating the latter to the former. So Hosea was able to assert on behalf of Israel's God: "It was *I* who gave [them] the grain, the wine, and the oil [italics supplied]" (2:8). In every instance of Baalistic infiltration into Israel's true faith, the prophets reacted vigorously and realistically. They displayed an intelligent awareness of the perspective of their audiences and of the peculiar nature of the gospel that they brought to bear upon it. In this way it was possible for them really to communicate what they had to say and to secure genuine responses.

The similarity of this situation to that which can be presently observed should be noted. Our culture contains elements which are related to Christianity in its classical historical expression. This is wistfully and even nostalgically recognized by students of contemporary life and thought. There once *was* Christ, Calvary, the Pentecost, sacrificial love, the hope of a kingdom of God. Men once took these seriously, not only in church, but in education, government, and art.

But then came the extension of American frontiers, the conquest of nature, the exploitation of nature's resources, and the machine age. The general standard of living shot up with meteoric speed. The goods which men possessed in undreamed-of quantities and the machines that produced them became the gods which they adored. By these goods and these gods success was measured. To defend them and the freedom to have them, all resources must be mobilized, even those of the Christian religion. So God and the church may become servants of the state and of the economy, acting alongside its armies and jet planes to defend what men have.

The preservation of this flourishing economic way of life and of a democratic political society preoccupies Christian people. This makes it increasingly difficult for them to distinguish between the sovereign authority of God and the sovereign claims of the political and economic community. They confess in their creeds God's transcendent righteousness. But they admit in their workaday philosophy that they are seeking first man's kingdom rather than God's. An enlightened and highly sensitive materialism has arisen. This materialism is based on the abundance of goods and possession of the power to produce more goods rather than on a faith that was born in Palestine. It is not as crass probably as that which prevailed in ancient Palestine, but it is as rampant and as inimical to true religion as it was in the time of the great prophets.

Accordingly the modern prophet has the task of his early predecessors—the utilization of the values of the secularized pseudo Christianity of his time and the defense of the peculiar essentials of the faith that he has received as a Christian preacher called of God. A flat rejection of the former, even to the extent of refusal to use its terminology in communicating the latter, will cut him off from his generation and congregation. Much more important, it will render him utterly incapable of acting as a spokesman of God to his day since he will be talking in a language that is strange to his people's ears. His people's perspective must be his, so that his mind and theirs will have a common meeting ground. This does not mean, of course, that he will betray his Lord and adopt the secular gods which are rivals of the true faith. It may mean that he will learn from his generation and its culture insights and techniques which he may use in the service of the gospel.

He, like the preachers of Israel, must continually turn to the source of his faith and refresh his mind and heart in the wonder of its truth. This theological and personally spiritual exercise enables the prophets again and again to identify the great realities in which they believe. It gives them the power to declare unequivocally the distinctive and redemptive nature of their faith.

So we must turn to the theological perspective of the prophets. It was in the name of this faith that they repudiated the Baalism of their day and sought to turn the people to the God of Israel. The special characteristics of this faith emerged as the prophets preached in the various crises of the nation's life.

The prophetic books are important sources for our knowledge of the biblical faith and theology. What the prophets believed is not divorced from the general viewpoint in the Old Testament. It is integral therewith. We need to understand the religious beliefs of the prophets for two reasons: first, these beliefs are a prominent part of their message; and second, they are central in the books of the Bible, which is held by the church to be the revealed Word of God, containing the gospel of man's salvation.

We are concerned both to understand how and what the prophets preached and also to emulate them in the forceful declaration of their biblical Word of deliverance. This purpose is obviously related to the preacher's needs, but it does not suffice. The problem goes much deeper than theological content and persuasive speech. It lies in the general orientation of the minister toward the Bible. Too often he sees it as a source book of homiletical material. Until he comes to an experience of the Bible which has the impact upon him of an I-Thou encounter, he will fail to comprehend the meaning of the prophetic faith for himself.

The Bible contains the saving Word of God which is directed to each man. Its teachings and principles are meaningless abstractions until they penetrate his conscience with radical personal relevance and disturbing force. When this penetration occurs, the words of the Bible become luminous with meaning. The words become useful in their theological context for articulating and formalizing the experience of God that the Bible has made possible. When this happens to the modern prophet, he has not only a personal knowledge of God but a shared knowledge. The Scripture he uses and to a great degree the theological terms with which he interprets it come from the community of faith, the church. The prophet of Israel shared the faith of the chosen community which was the forerunner and foundation of the church of Christ. He preached the gospel which had been revealed to this community. This gospel is recorded in the books of the Old Testament.

The successor to the prophets of Israel cannot escape the responsibility of sharing creatively the faith of the Christian community. He must enunciate their gospel as this was fulfilled in Christ. In a word, his theological perspective must in a profound way be in harmony with theirs.

What was the faith of the prophets? A theological position is seldom consciously argued, because this was not the purpose of these men. Yet it constitutes the solid structure of their thought which they usually take for granted and use as the intellectual framework for their preaching. Unless the reader of their sermons knows what this position is, he will be unable to follow their argument or understand its real significance. Their speeches are not reasoned discourses. They do not develop the presuppositions which lie behind them. They are passionate outbursts uttered under the provocation of immediate situations. But behind these outbursts lies a consistent, highly impressive, and strikingly distinctive theology.

It has been stated earlier that the prophet-preacher received his call and his power to preach from God. He became a problem to his people because he insisted on speaking the truth which God revealed to him. This truth of revelation was not generalized truth about religion or the nature of ultimate reality. It was truth of a special kind, related specifically to the nature and will of the God of the prophets.

We must know about this God, what he has done in history for man's salvation, as only a prophetic preacher can reveal this. We must learn his purpose for men in their life on earth, as only the prophet's word can indicate it. With the prophets we must become aware of what he is that we may worship him and glorify his holy name.

First, the God of Amos, Isaiah, Hosea, Micah, Jeremiah, was the supreme Lord of history. In his sight the nations were as a drop in the bucket. But his compassion included them as well as his people Israel. Over against the gods of Canaan, associated with the fertility cult, Israel's God was the prime mover of events, the determiner of the fate of nations, and the protector of his people. At the beginning of creation he began to realize his purpose for men by creating them, setting them in families and nations, and indicating to them the nature of their obligation to him. The God of Israel was not impersonal force, a life principle within the natural process, or a ritualistic symbol to be used in worship only. He was dynamic purpose, personal power, transcendent holiness, with which every act and plan of man had to reckon. He alone could guarantee the success of the human enterprise. For this reason he was called the living God.

The prophets reacted vigorously to this living God whose Word they must proclaim. They were concerned with living, concrete situations to which the divine action needed to be directed. They revealed in their preaching an understanding of the God who acts and of man who is required to respond. The prophet's encounter with this living God made him vividly aware that God lived and that he challenged all human life to acknowledge his power and authority.

Here again, the perspective of the prophet calls for comparison with the present situation of the preacher. Between him and the living God are many intervening and distracting forces and powers, any or all of which claim to control the human situation. The living God is separated from living men by this intricate hierarchy of intermediate but potent values—machines, scientific techniques, political power, impersonal forces of nature, social pressure, group conflicts, and many other means of controlling man's life. If one or more of these is magnified by experienced proof of its effectiveness, the nature and action of the living God becomes all the more remote and irrelevant. To confess and proclaim him to men becomes all the more imperative, especially in the face of much evidence that secondary controls lead to despair.

Further, the living Lord of history to whom the prophets had surrendered their lives and wills was altogether righteous. He was the supreme source of human good and of a good whose greatness human beings could hardly imagine, so wonderful and terrible were its dimensions. Beyond all the power manifested in nature, beyond the power structures erected by men, and beyond everything in the supernatural spiritual order stood the splendor of the righteousness of God. It was not a righteousness in the presence of which they stood with paralyzing awe, although this was not completely absent from the experience of the prophets. It was a penetrating, challenging, empowering righteousness which possessed and energized them into effective action. It filled the whole earth, but in particular it filled the mind and soul of the prophet. This caused his speech to become a flaming, searing sword, penetrating the consciences of men and laying bare their sin in the sight of

God. It was this divine righteousness to realize which the God of Israel entered the history of his people.

Wonderful and terrible as this righteousness was, it had been made known to men as justice in their various relationships. Men must seek justice and live! The life which could result from this quest for God's justice was granted by God in his mercy. It was not the automatic result of conformity with some moral law. The benefits of goodness, therefore, the prophets believed, came through the direct, personal action of God. But the great benefit lay in the part that man's obedience played in restoring man to God's favor on the basis of repentance and reconciliation. So the power of God's righteousness is a redemptive power for individuals and for entire communities. For this reason the prophets addressed their words of condemnation to every kind of human situation, insisting on a response to God's righteous will.

The prophet always demands that every form of human goodness be judged by the God of eternal righteousness. He discovered that the goodness that God demanded was not the goodness of moral achievement on the level of human history. His ways were not their ways, nor were his thoughts about righteousness man's thoughts. So the prophet's perspective enabled him to distinguish between the ethical systems of men and the revealed righteousness that came from above. The prophet, no matter what his personal feelings in the matter, could not confuse the two or use the latter to sanctify the former.

At this point the modern prophet faces one of his greatest difficulties. How can he communicate the word of God's righteousness to men who are righteous in their own eyes and through their own moral effort? Even those forms of human and historical morality which have been affected by Christian ethics—perhaps especially these forms—are shot through with elements of human pride and desire for power, so that they seem almost impervious to the Word of condemnation in the name of God.

Then the God of the prophet is known to be the altogether righteous Lord of history through the fact that he is Revealer and Redeemer. The God who is a revealer must possess personal will and compassionate love as the source and motive for his revealing action. He does not reveal for the purpose of imparting truth. His purpose is to give himself in the form of regenerating, purifying power for the sake of his sinning creatures. The fact of his revelation clearly distinguishes God's salvation from human substitutes.

The ways of revelation should not be minimized, but the *fact* must ever be foremost. The prophets never allowed the people to forget this as they proclaimed the Word of their God. They accepted the common view that God communicated his will to his people through dreams, visions, nature, history, and tradition. But they were deeply convinced that a response to revelation in ethical-personal-community terms was demanded. This, they believed, was far more important than an analysis of the manner in which it was delivered to men.

The Bible's interest in revelation through special events of history is of particular significance. The God of the prophets is a God who acts for the deliverance of men. He is made known to them through this action. Thus history assumes an extraordinary importance in the Bible and especially in the thought of the prophets. History is not fully described by a recital of events. Its real meaning is found in the relation of God's purpose to special events which he initiates—the Exodus, the Exile, the Restoration, and finally the event of Christ, his birth, life, death, resurrection, and coming again. In these may be seen the true nature of God and the redemptive nature of his revelation.

It is the problem and the task of the preacher today, if he is to proclaim the Word of salvation which transcends yet includes history, to relate this biblical view to the common-sense conception of his congregation. To do this, he himself must make a personal commitment to the former. Generally speaking, the modern view consists of recognition of a series of events occurring on the two-dimensional level of time and space. These events sustain a cause-effect relationship to one another. They occur because of the operation of economic-political and personal forces in their relation to the processes and resources of nature. That they are used by God or have a real bearing upon man's final deliverance from evil is not logically connected with this modern view.

A further and indispensable aspect of the prophet's idea of God may be considered before we turn to his view of man. This is the conception of God's holiness. The prophets proclaimed the rational, righteous, personal character of God. Yet this characteristic of holiness stands out conspicuously in the preaching and in the theological assumptions of the prophet. It is difficult to find suitable synonyms for this term. The power that it suggests, however, may be stated in simple language. God's power is holy, that is, beyond the capacity of men to emulate or create. It is manifested in his triumphant control of history. It is present also in his redemptive judgment of men and societies no matter how firm their resistance to his will. His use of the forces of nature to achieve his goals for mankind also demonstrates his holiness. It is evident in those biblical passages in which it signifies or clearly implies the transcendence of God's power over human weakness and limitations.

It is the best term for identifying the uniqueness and the

distinctiveness of the divine nature so that it can never be confused with man's. The term suggests a nonrational element, a mysterious and indefinable power which fills men with wonder and arouses in them the impulse to adoration and worship. Beyond everything that God has made known about himself to men, there is the unknown and unrevealed. Yet prophetic preaching was concerned with what men could do because of their sin on the basis of God's *revealed* requirements. But the very preaching carried overtones of mystery, awe, and worship of the majestic God whose holiness filled the whole earth, as well as the place of worship.

Once more, the bearing of this upon the viewpoint and action of the preacher today must be indicated. God's holiness, for example, is a perpetual warning against deifying man's goodness and virtue. God may never be constructed by the mind of man into the image of man. His essential nature resists man's effort to search for the divine in the universe and then to create a God out of his findings. The only way to formulate a statement about God which is true is to base it upon what has been revealed in Scripture. Apart from this basis men's definitions of God may move in any one of hundreds of directions. None of these can provide a substitute for the redemptive action of the God of Israel who was in Christ. Numerous aberrations and eccentricities in theology and religion exist in the Christian world today. They illustrate the futility of their non-biblical and nonprophetic approach to the meaning of God. Only as the living, righteous, holy God confronts him in Scripture and in life can the preacher declare the effective Word of salvation to his people. Indeed, apart from this God he can never become a prophet.

Turn now to the prophet's conception of the human creature. As in the case of the prophet of old, so with respect to the modern prophet his view of man is more adequately reflected by the way he treats him in sermon and pastoral relations than in any formal statement or doctrine.

Certainly of primary importance is the fact of man's creation by the act and intention of God. The manner of this creation hardly concerned the prophets, nor need it concern us here. The prophet preached upon the assumption that man is a creature whose creation brings him into a special and highly disturbing relation to his Maker. As a creature of this God man is dependent upon him for all that he is and has. His fate is thus in the hands of God, as are his thoughts, his hopes, his dreams, and his fears, As a creature he is fearfully weak, sharing a frustrating mortality with every other living thing. As a creature he is prone to compensate for his weakness by strenuous struggle to achieve independence from his Maker.

Thus man is a sinner. He reveals this when he refuses to accept his dependence upon God and sets his will against God's. God in his mercy has endowed man with true selfhood, or the capacity to achieve it. Man is therefore free to pursue this goal also. As a person made in the divine image he is capable of becoming a son of God. Man reaches out in his world for the extension of his freedom. He uses it to conquer its resources for his own advantage. As a creature, however, he knows he is of the earth, earthy. He resembles the animals who were also made out of the dust of the ground. He directs his energies in a constant attempt to forget his origin. He tries to live down this lowly and humiliating beginning by defying his Maker and trying to wield power which is not his to wield.

His chief sin therefore is pride. He asserts himself by promoting his favorite projects in an all-out effort to make himself into God, who alone is Creator. He takes God's permissive command "Have dominion!" literally and forgets the limitation his creation places upon all his capacities and resources. To such a man the prophets preached—to sinners flaunting their power and possessions and attainments. He preached to men who proudly proclaimed the superiority of their particular practices and beliefs, and insisted upon accepting no criterion save their own for evaluating their way of life. The prophets implied that man is also endowed with personhood and the capacity for repentance, faith, and a new life. To such a man the prophets preached with hope.

The seat of man's sin is his willful rebellion against God and against his purpose for men. This is *sin* not sins, the sin of self-glorification and unfounded pride. Such sin makes it possible for men to commit the so-called overt sins which are often confused with radical sin residing in the will of man. This is the fundamental sin which the prophets attacked.

They saw the power of collective sin. They noted how this took the form of institutional group pride. They did not ignore the outer manifestations of this inner sin among men, although they condemned the latter with particular vehemence. Collective denials of God's sovereignty, such as forms of nationalism, economic life, and political order, were brought under their severe condemnation. They were unable to think of sin in purely individualistic categories or to abstract the sinning individual from the context of his society. At this point the modern prophet must learn from the prophets of Israel, even though it may mean the abandonment of cherished conceptions and attitudes.

The Hebrew prophets shared the general view of their time that a man belonged to his community, his family, his tribe, and his nation. This belonging was cultural, social, political, ethical, psychological, and religious. Thus it seemed to be complete and unqualified. From his birth biblical man accepted

101

and was conditioned by this fact of his community. It was potent in the enforcement of criminal law, marriage practices, moral codes, and religious beliefs. The prophets found in this social psychology the basis for the enunciation of a gospel of freedom which became normative for the outlook of the entire Bible, not excepting the New Testament. They received from the tradition of Israel the concept of the covenant community, that is to say, the chosen people, a concept which was the central concern of their entire ministry. This concept is so crucial for understanding the preaching of the prophets that some of its features should be sketched briefly. The fact that this concept is so generally misunderstood or ignored by Christian people lends weight to this effort.

Going back to traditions which date as early as the time of the judges (Judg. 5), if not the time of Moses, Israel considered herself to be the people of the covenant, a covenant she had entered into through her ancestors. Through this covenant she received the divine promise of protection and blessing, and she responded with an oath of allegiance. In this way Israel became the covenant people, the chosen nation. Her history gave her many opportunities to distort the true meaning of her call and to seek her own ends and goals. Her religious leaders, and especially the prophets, kept reminding her of the need for faithfulness to the terms of the covenant.

The true covenant community was not identical with the nation; but it was rather the congregation or people of God, who served their Lord by their faith, their worship, and their obedience to his revealed will. Theirs was the duty of obeying him and of witnessing faithfully, even painfully, to his love and righteousness, so that all nations might glorify the God of Israel. The covenant community was the true Church, the called-out faithful, bound to their Redeemer rather than to the demands of the world. In this community of faith the individual discovered that his salvation and true freedom were intimately associated with the salvation and welfare of the whole.

He also learned that the practice of true community as this was stipulated by God in Scripture and through the prophets did not destroy him as an individual. Indeed, it permitted the emergence and development of his highest manhood; in fact, demanded it. The conflict between the individual and society readily produces a dehumanized mass man. In the community of faith are found the conditions which preserve both for the service of their Creator.

The covenant community, which constituted the frame of reference for prophetic preaching, was the true Church in which each member found his fulfillment and salvation. This community was continued in the New Testament, as the early Christian writings abundantly confirm. Jesus, the disciples, and early Christian leaders were fully aware that this was so. It is well when the modern Christian preacher learns this fact of the nature of the true Church. Then he is alive to the relation of his preaching to the true Church and to its historical form—Methodist, Anglican, Presbyterian, Baptist, as the case may be. And the prophet, contrary to a rather common understanding of his role, belongs to the community of faith and preaches its word of reconciliation and renewal. He is not a lone wolf or a solitary malcontent, unhappy about organized religion in group form. He is the interpreter of the divine meaning of group faith on the basis of the covenant which came to Israel and of the far-reaching implications of its theology.

The foregoing discussion has prepared us for a final word with respect to the prophet's theological perspective, namely, the meaning of salvation. This meaning has an integral relation to what God and man and sin are. Here too the modern prophet misses the peculiarly biblical view of sin and salvation at his peril. Both belong to the total gospel which he has been called to preach. The God of the prophets is the Savior of mankind. Because of his own unmerited love he took action to bring salvation to men.

He sought the well-being of his people in many ways—the transformation of their inner lives, the provision of physical welfare and prosperity, and the regeneration of their attitudes and relations. In a word, the total life of the entire community was to be restored according to his righteous will. Salvation is the *complete good that God could and would bring to his creatures.* It is not a limited good, confined to particular individuals, to particular areas of their lives, or to existence after the end of earthly life. It is inclusive of all these but seeks the perfect fulfillment of God's purpose in history and beyond history.

Salvation is initiated and controlled by the Redeemer upon whose acts man is completely dependent. God takes the initiative, and man makes the response that is called for. "Seek the Lord, that you may live," Amos cried (5:6 Amer. Trans.). He thus laid upon the nation and its leaders the burden of reforming its policies and programs so as to bring them into harmony with the will of God. Amos and the other great prophets as well were firmly convinced that men *may* seek the Lord. By so doing they would have life and they would have it more abundantly. We should note the height and breadth and depth of this view of salvation. The whole nation in all its relations is to repent and turn to God. It must purify and reorient its economic practices, judicial procedures, habits of worship at the shrine, and even its thought about the day of judgment. The purging fires of God's wrath and the restoring power of his merciful love must touch every facet of the community's life.

Salvation reaches into the nation's department of state also and promises historical vindication for international policies which derive from trust in the Lord of history. The modern student may not take literally for his own day the specific advice which some of the prophets gave to ruling kings. Still it is important to note that they did give advice and made strong recommendations on foreign policy in the name of their God. Theirs was no emaciated, withdrawn religion, fit only for a hermit's cell or for an individual seeking the removal of anxiety neuroses. It was a conquering, all-embracing faith which searched out and redeemed every nook and corner of human existence, every motive and custom of men.

Yet the inner core of salvation was the affirmative answer that man made when God sought him out and aroused his faith. This encounter was the heart of the matter for the prophets and should be for us who are their successors. When a man cries out, "Woe is me!" and then finally replies to God's invitation, "Here I am!" he learns the wonder of his redemption and at the same time the solemnity of his obligation to his community which God has also redeemed. To seek this experience for himself and for his people is the great objective of the prophet whom God has called. This is the meaning of salvation for the prophet.

I have sketched the nature and indicated the challenge of the cultural and theological perspective of the prophet of Israel. I have also emphasized the bearing of this perspective upon that of the prophet today, pointing out certain similarities between the two. This has been done in the belief that no understanding of the prophets is possible without ascertaining their peculiar viewpoint. We must at least be aware of this if we are to comprehend what they were doing and why they were trying to do it.

But more than this has been attempted in this chapter. This discussion has sought to show how we may emulate the prophets and use them and their perspective. They provide a criterion for an honest and thorough re-examination of our preaching experience. It is our obligation to study their position and use it, not only as a provocative stimulus, but as a norm, because it represents the very heart of the faith recorded in the Bible. This faith must be formulated afresh in the language of each generation. Such a formulation must have symbols for faithfully communicating the biblical understanding of God and man, sin and salvation. Without this understanding prophetic preaching is impossible. If it is not honestly present, preaching must be renamed and its purpose redefined.

VI

The Prophet's Proclamation

WHAT SHALL THE PROPHET PREACH, AND HOW SHALL HE PHRASE and deliver his message to his people? The casual reading of the church news section of the Saturday paper published in any large city will reveal that there is little or no agreement as to the essential content of the sermon, if titles are any criterion. These will run the entire gamut of religious interest, from peace of mind to convulsions marking the end of the world. This question with its twofold concern can be answered only by coming to grips with the nature of normative prophetic preaching as set forth in the Bible. The prophet selects his themes, formulates his ideas, and delivers his sermon on the basis of his passionate commitment to the covenant God of justice and mercy. This dedication to the supreme task of communicating the redemptive Word of this God in all its glory and power radically determines both the content and the manner of his proclamation.

In an ancient situation a prophet who stood alone retorted to fellow prophets who preferred to stand for the wishes of their ruler, in these words: "What the Lord says to me, that I will speak" (I Kings 22:14). He had no word which was drawn from the fears and ambitions of his contemporaries. His word was God's, received by revelation to the prophet as he humbly and courageously waited for it in the midst of his people. With respect to each sermon the prophet must be able to say with Ezekiel, "The word of the Lord came to me." Without this assurance the prophet has no message from God, and without a message from God the prophet is merely a lecturer to an audience. But this Word which he is required to preach is a Word for man's total redemption, and thus it has authority and meaning for every area of human life on all levels of man's existence.

It is a Word directed to health of mind and body, to the production and distribution of material goods. Its healing power encompasses also society and its forms of organization, political life and international relations. Personal habits and moral standards are to come under its judgment. To all of these the gospel of the prophetic preacher has a penetrating and inescapable relevance. Consequently the problem of what to preach becomes the problem of what not to preach, so pressing and endlessly insistent are the demands that the life of his people makes upon the dedicated man of God in the pulpit. A few of the life situations to which the prophets addressed themselves when they preached will show what they thought to be important and how they related the revealed Word to the special problems of the community which they served.

First of all, the prophets could never avoid reckoning with the problem of national survival. Very few sermons failed to take this serious question into account. Passionately devoted to the land of their fathers, Israel's prophets had no desire to dodge this issue. And as the nation moved toward the day of her defeat, the prophets were increasingly preoccupied with the problems for religious faith which its imminence created. Military crises were common for this economically and technologically weak nation, located between mighty empires. She was as constantly threatened with destruction as were the small states located between Germany and Russia in World War II.

Unavoidably then the prophets preached on the theme of survival, but in their own distinctive way. To them survival meant the nation's obedience to the purpose of God as revealed in her covenant history. Examples of prophetic preaching in this type of situation are readily found in the Old Testament. The great prophets tried to save the nation by announcing its coming destruction, for example. This strange approach can be seen in the preaching of Amos. Having aroused the interest of his listeners by promising the overthrow of the enemies of their nation—Syria (Damascus), Philistia (Gaza), Ammon, and Moab—the preacher suddenly announced the downfall of Israel herself (2:6). When this verbal bombshell burst in their midst, the people were totally unprepared for its coming. The element of surprise may have made them more receptive to the ethical and religious impact of his message. It is probable that the prophet was not thinking of any particular nation as the conqueror of Israel. He was primarily concerned for the moral regeneration of the life of the whole national community. His ethical interest is evident in his explanation of the defeat that is at hand—perversion of justice, indifference to the plight of the needy, exploitation of the poor.

In this instance the Word which the prophet preached was one of moral judgment aimed at repentance on a national scale, although this result is implied rather than positively stated. National defeat is viewed as the consequence of disobedience to the righteous God. Committed completely to this God, Amos preached furiously and vehemently in his name. This can hardly be called negative preaching, unless a fierce proclamation of the sovereign authority of a God who is altogether righteous and an announcement of the certainty of his judgment against the unrighteous are negative preaching. It may be harsh and painful preaching, but it forthrightly manifests the concern of God for the righteousness which must be the cornerstone of every nation and people.

Another prophet who related his sermons to the national crisis with vigor and effectiveness is Micah. After an introduction rich in poetic imagery (believed by some critics to be editorial) the speaker plunged into his subject. He bluntly announced the doom which was about to overtake Israel and Judah, twin kingdoms which alike had earned what was coming to them. After declaring that destruction was at hand, Micah expressed his own agony over the fate which was to befall his people. His pain-filled words must have deeply impressed his audience, even though they may not have been moved to change their ways. He identified the reason for the coming evil in concrete ways—a consuming greed for possessions, the exclusion from their homes of small farmers with its disruption of the traditional land economy. This was evil in the sight of God, who would send the conqueror in judgment upon Israel. This illustration of Micah's preaching again shows the correlation between deliverance from the ravages of war and deliverance from the sin of injustice, cruelty, and greed through repentance and the enthronement of righteousness in the life of the nation. If Micah declared that

Zion shall be plowed like a field,
And Jerusalem shall become a ruin (Jer. 26:18 Amer. Trans.).

because of the venality and inhumanity of her priests, prophets, judges, and rulers, he surely meant also that Zion shall be preserved if leaders and people turn wholeheartedly to God.

It is evident from the examples mentioned above that national survival was not the chief aim of the preaching which Israel's prophets carried on. Theirs was a greater interest derived from a knowledge of the purpose of their God for his people. The frank acceptance, not without great agony of spirit, of the coming of disaster marked their preaching when they encountered stubbornly entrenched iniquity in the community.

Examples of this kind of preaching could be multiplied, but we should now consider the significance which it has for the preacher in the twentieth century. Can he be truly a prophetic proclaimer of the Word of divine justice and judgment to his own nation? Certainly this kind of preaching involves a profound concern for the survival of his nation. But much more, it involves the glorification of the moral sovereignty of his God. This is a hard saying, but the first of these interests is clearly subordinated to the second in the prophet's preaching. Otherwise the natural urge to survive and its accompanying demand upon religious leaders to adjust their preaching to "national interests" may transform the preacher into a puppet of the state.

We may find it easy to understand the problem of the religious leaders of Israel when they were faced by this kind of situation. We may even admire their courage as they set themselves against the shortsighted leaders of the community in their proclamation of the righteous will of Israel's God. It is another matter to hold fast to the prophetic faith and to preach prophetically when we live in a national community that is neither weak nor notably humble. Yet it is impossible to reject the conclusion that preaching which does not realistically face the relation between national survival and God's moral demands is not biblical preaching at all.

What does the prophet preach *after* the predicted ruin has come and the nation ceases to have an independent existence? Does he gloat over the vindication of his authority as a predicter, or does he give way to profound grief over the fate of his nation? The answer is that he does neither if he is a true prophet. Rather he searches his heart and his religious consciousness for an understanding of the unhappy events which have transpired. He needs to learn how they are related to the fact of the living God whom he serves. This reaction is evident in the poems which are usually ascribed to the so-called Second Isaiah. This prophet-poet was the preacher to a community of people who had been forcibly removed from their homeland, the exiles in Babylonia. He had in his "congregation" the children of Jews who had actually lived through the experiences of the siege of Jerusalem and had endured the painfully humiliating defeat which concluded it. What could this prophet say to a people who had been taught that Zion was the city of their God and that his power to protect them was invincible? The grim fact of defeat cruelly contradicted this faith and threatened to destroy it. Here was the supreme test of his effectiveness as a prophet of God. When history and faith are in sharp conflict, which will win?

The prophet observed, and strongly reacted against, the acceptance of the victory of history by many of his people. They succumbed to the logic of events and turned away from the faith of their fathers. On the other hand, the prophet responded to the logic of his faith and preached a gospel which met the problem head on. This gospel, as has been indicated, involved the acceptance of the reality and power of the living God of history, actively engaged in directing its movement for his redemptive purposes. For this reason, tragic as they were in their consequences for Israel, historical events were always viewed in the light of God's purposeful action. He rather than history had the last word always.

Reflecting over these aspects of his faith, the prophet to the exiles composed an amazing sermon poem which he addressed to his people (Isa. 52–53). With graphic illustration and deep feeling he declared that the exiles must accept the implications of their destiny as a people of God. They must assume the role of a suffering servant, despised and rejected of men but gladly enduring misfortune that other nations might be redeemed. (The writer grants that the conception of the servant used here is but one of several possible views.) This astonishing pronouncement flatly opposed popular and deeply entrenched views of national destiny. It was repugnant to patriotic feeling. It would have received no acceptance whatsoever had Israel not already suffered humiliating defeat and the bitterness of exile. Supporting the prophet in his radical view of Israel's destiny was the impact of previous prophetic teaching. This teaching had always reminded Israel of her peculiar destiny to be a people of God rather than a nation competing with other nations. Her tragedy was her inability to disentangle herself from the involvements of national life sufficiently to devote herself to her obligations as a community of faith.

In his sermon the Second Isaiah described the fate of the faithful nation by declaring that stripes, deformity, ugliness, wounds, rejection, and judgment would be its lot. Incredibly he rejected the goals and ideals toward which nations customarily set their course. Victory, prosperity, a sense of superiority over other nations, are the ends they seek. What strange distortion of national destiny did the prophet seek to produce? we may well ask. Was he not fantastically out of touch with political reality and with the temper of his times? But when we recall the character of the true prophet's commitment and call, his teaching does not seem to be so fantastic, after all. He was really completely in touch with reality and the deepest meaning of the gospel—its Word of world redemption through patient and obedient suffering on the part of the community of faith. The God of Israel had one supreme purpose in history—so to direct his people that they might faithfully witness before all men to the wonder of his redeeming love. When the historical fortunes of his people were at low ebb and the cup of their humiliation was being drunk to its last bitter dregs, God was in fact using them as the victorious instrument of his love for the nations of the world.

The preacher in our time is obligated to adapt this profound teaching to the situation in which his people find themselves. He needs to be on his guard lest he find no parallel or so "spiritualize" the biblical passage as to make it irrelevant to the life of the national community. It is true that the people who constitute the Church rather than the entire nation are his congregation. But they are at the same time citizens of a country. He cannot ignore the relations and obligations which they sustain to the latter. Since the word of the prophet has an inclusive outreach, it speaks to the citizen as well as to the worshiper in the Church. It tells him that God alone is sovereign, that ultimate success depends upon acceptance of his will and way, and that this involves humble repentance, the confession of sin, and a life of righteousness. The Christian citizen must accept this way for himself and bend every effort to secure its acceptance and application in the collective life of the community, both local and national.

The fact that this Christian way runs counter to what is called the way of patriotism will not dishearten the true prophet of God. Patriotism itself must be judged and redeemed by his preaching of the prophetic Word. The nation must hear this Word of the supreme Lord of all mankind. Through it his demand for the grateful practice of love and justice by his human creatures will be heard. This Word announces that God alone is supreme and that the pretense of any nation, including the prophet's, to be its own final judge of conduct and ideals is sinful, idolatrous, and ultimately disastrous. The modern prophet, like Second Isaiah, will urge his nation to be compassionate and sacrificial in sharing with others. He will point to the fact that suffering of this sort has a healing and redeeming function whereby the nations may at last learn to live together under God.

But more directly and intimately, the prophet will preach to his people as a people of God, who are called out of the world to be his true Church and to demonstrate his purpose for men by their faith and their obedience to his will. By being the true Church in this manner, they can make known to the world the meaning of true community for every kind of human relationship. In being the true Church, the people of the prophet may in a peculiar way exemplify how God wants all men to live—on the basis of love, forgiveness, repentance, holiness, and faith. They will manifest this to one another in the Church and in the society in which it is set. By closing its ranks and staying close to its Lord, such a church, Second Isaiah confidently asserts, will arouse first astonishment, then wonder, and finally acceptance of its way by the world.

So this great prophet handles the problem of preaching the Word of justice and judgment to his nation by preaching the Word of faith and obedient suffering to the Church. Beyond the social and political action its members may take is the spiritual orientation of faith and love which God demands of them. Through such an adjustment they will be properly motivated for the action they will feel called to take as Chris-

115

tian citizens of a political community. And through such an adjustment they will be able to transform every form of defeat into a spiritual victory. This conception of his task will not be easy on the prophet nor on the people in the pews of his church, but it is the only view compatible with his high calling.

Also prominent in prophetic preaching is the theme of injustice in the social order in which his people live and make their living. The prophets were capable of intense anger when they saw exploitation, cruelty, and injustice in the community which they so painfully loved. Stern and relentless were their frequent condemnations of social evil. Their attack was vigorous and direct, aimed at specific examples of evil, although at times general ethical principles were enunciated also. They believed that the only valid defense for the nation, when it was threatened by external foes, was an ethical and spiritual one. This defense took the form of humble penitence and complete obedience to the righteous God of Israel. The prophets stressed this again and again, turning the searing flames of God's righteous wrath against the centers and leaders of corruption in the life of the nation. No group or class was exempt from this attack. Landowners, judges, businessmen, political leaders, even prophets and priests, as well as the whole nation, were compelled to hear it.

When the prophets condemned landowners, they did not attack these as a class. Only those who were intent on foreclosing mortgages and seizing the land of the small farmer were denounced. The prophets of the eighth century lived in a period of a radical shift in the land economy. Large landowners were flourishing at the expense of the owners of small holdings. (For the previous century the dramatic account of Elijah's rebuke of King Ahab for the latter's seizure of Naboth's vineyard [I Kings 21] suggests that this change was already under way.) Micah and Isaiah were incensed by the greed of these men (Mic. 2:1-2; Isa. 5:8). They protested primarily against this evidence of consuming greed because it contradicted the demands of their God for justice. They saw in this shift also a threat to the ancestral system of land control in Israel. Such greed seals its own doom:

> Woe to those who join house to house,
>   who add field to field,
> until there is no more room.

Unchecked by a regard for personal and social values, their lust for power was a shocking perversion of God's purpose for his people. Like the landowners, judges who could be bought had become blind to the high role they were called to play in society in preserving justice for each man against tyranny and crime.

> They [the judges] sell the righteous for silver,
>   and the needy for a pair of shoes. (Amos 2:6.)

This corruption of the judiciary strikes at the very heart of the community which is called to do justly and to love mercy, for a judge was directly bound by rules of impartiality and equity in the performance of his office (Isa. 5:23).

Men engaged in business and trade were also denounced by the prophets. They were consumed with such longing to carry on their business that they became impatient when a holy day interrupted their pursuit of gain (Amos 2:5). They not only despised the sacred days, but they were not willing to use them for the purpose of worshiping the God obedience to whom demands the practice of righteousness. Without this restraint upon their conduct they trampled upon the needy and destroyed the poor. When their God looked for justice, he heard only the cries of oppressed men, says Isaiah, with an impressive play on words not apparent in a translation of the original Hebrew (5:7). The rulers of Israel shared in this general disregard for justice which was bringing the nation to destruction. They "hate the good and love the evil." With a vivid figure Micah referred to their cruelty as cannibalism (3:2-3). So it was not strange that even the religious leaders were self-seeking, ostensibly trusting in the Lord, but actually trusting in their own bag of tricks to boost their collection (Mic. 3:11)!

Illustrations of the prophet's attack upon injustice cited above reveal his unrelenting repudiation of this social and personal evil. He composes no learned essays on social questions; he minces no words. Forceful, passionate, pointed, his barbed sentences strike home, no matter where he aims them. He lashes out at the evil motives and passions of men, exposing their cruelty and baseness. Earnestly he calls for a reorientation of life based on loyalty to the true God of Israel. Because of this penetrating spiritual and psychological discernment, the prophet was no mere proponent of social and economic reforms. Because these revealed an inner disorientation, the prophet was concerned with every indication of undedicated passion and unredeemed self-interest which could be found in his community. Among these he noted in addition to many examples of injustice forms of sensuality which were highly respectable and intimately connected with the contemporary culture. These he condemned from his typical viewpoint, a viewpoint which, as will be indicated shortly, is seldom found in moralistic sermons on sensuality in our day. Observing the spiritual and social desolation which had been created in his day by unchecked greed and lust, Jeremiah is compelled to speak out. He cries:

I am full of the wrath of the Lord;
I am weary of holding it in.

.   .   .   .

From the least to the greatest of them,
every one is greedy for unjust gain. (6:11, 13.)

Additional illustrations of prophetic preaching on the general theme of sensuality will be illuminating for the modern preacher, especially if his church has a Puritan tradition in its history. One form of evil which they handled in their sermons was the use of intoxicating drink. This problem baffles many a modern preacher because of its moralistic implications and the differences of opinion in his church as to its "sinfulness." The prophetic approach to this problem is highly significant for contemporary preaching. The prophet Isaiah (5:11-12, 22-23) clarified the issue as to the evil of drinking when he denounced those who sought strong drink all day long but did not see the work of the Lord, that is, were blind to his activity in history. Such men held positions of responsibility in the community. They probably were judges, described as "heroes at drinking wine," "who acquit the guilty for a bribe." Drunken revelries, aggravated by the insatiable thirst and gluttony of wealthy women, involved reclining on costly couches, gorging on meat, and guzzling wine out of large bowls. Participants in these orgies were not condemned because they drank. The prophet denounced them because their drinking made them intellectually and spiritually insensitive. They lost their capacity for sorrow over the imminent ruin of their country and for understanding its cause (Amos 4:1; 6:4-6) .

It is evident that the prophet had the profoundest of all reasons for his attack upon the use of alcoholic beverages—strong drink, wine, new wine. He had observed the personal rejection of God which such use involved. Hosea put it bluntly:

Wine and new wine
take away the understanding

. . . .

and they have left their God. (4:11, 12.)

Here is the real and radical reason as well as justification for
the prophet's attitude toward drinking and toward other forms
of sensuality as well. The prophet is called to proclaim the
gospel of redemption, a redemption which is possible only
through absolute devotion to the just and merciful God of
the covenant. Extreme sensitivity to the will of this God and
ready compliance with his demands are the true tests of devotion to him.

If men are to love him completely, they themselves must
be completely whole. Such completeness is impossible when
the gods of lust, sensuality, self-regard, and desire for power
determine their daily habits. Wine and worship of such a God
cannot mix; each demands man's all ultimately. Wine as used
in the preaching of the prophets is, of course, but one symbol
of the practical denial of God which is also present in other
absorbing forms of sensuality. By using the term "denial of
God," the biblical depth of this act is indicated. Rather than
denial on the level of doctrine or intellectual affirmation, this
biblical denial involves the actual existence, the attitudes, and
passions of man. These are organized around the self as their
center rather than God.

Thus the deep theological basis for the rejection of strong
drink as sinful is paramount for the prophet. Considerations
of a biological, psychological, and social nature must be subordinated to this primary meaning of God rejection. Consequently the prophetic preacher who considers whether or how
he should preach a temperance sermon needs to rethink the

whole matter, as do the Church's agencies which are interested especially in this problem. He is no prophet unless he is passionately dedicated to the task of revealing the will and the power of the altogether holy and righteous God, who is a jealous God. Beside him there can be no other—no personal god of self-will, personal power, lust, or passion. Temperance with respect to this supreme God or to these rivals is impossible. It is a question of preaching the *demanding* as well as the giving love of God, so that with a single heart, an undefiled body, a healthy nervous system, and a quickened spirit men may love him without reservation or lust-imposed limitation. There is no "temperance" in the Bible where devotion to God is concerned. Rather there is total dedication of life to him and total abstinence from everything that hinders or diminishes it.

Another type of situation which is reflected in the content of the prophets' sermons is that created by the popularity of religion in ancient Israel. This phenomenon characterizes our day as well as that of Israel's prophets. An inquiry into their preaching to such a situation may have considerable value for the preacher whose pews are crowded or who hopefully studies the techniques of some widely acclaimed modern evangelist.

As to Israel's prophets theirs was a day of faith, of crowds thronging the places of worship, of booming religion. The prophets spoke of the "multitude of your sacrifices," "trampling of [the] courts [of the Temple]," "solemn assembly," "all [the] men of Judah who [come] to worship" the God of Israel, "sacrifices every morning," offerings of "thousands of rams," and "ten thousands of rivers of oil." The prophets' contemporaries ascribed their prosperity to God and fixed their hope on him. They eagerly waited for the outpouring of even more blessings on the day of the Lord (Amos 5:18), which they believed was near. Confident that God was on their side—Was he not the

God of Israel?—they had nothing to fear and many comforts to enjoy. In gratitude—and the expectation of many favors to come, doubtless—they trampled the courts of the Lord. They delighted in the Temple liturgy. This may have had a quieting effect upon any uneasiness of conscience possibly aroused by the sight of filthy, starved beggars near the Temple's entrance. What did the prophets preach in this situation of flourishing religion and crowded sanctuaries (churches)? Did they hail it as a sign of a new day, a revival of religion, a return to God? Did they point with pride to the piety of national leaders as proof of a national revival?

It is certain that the true prophets did none of these things, for they saw clearly the real meaning of the current popularity of religion. They had seen God in the beauty and over-whelming glory of his holiness. By this God they had been called, and it was his Word that they had been commanded to preach—a Word of condemnation for the sin of pride and of reproach for the sins of injustice among men. They saw how complacency and self-righteousness were perverting Israel's faith in her living God, substituting the subject of this faith for its object. They saw how Israel made herself God, while retaining the illusion that she continued to worship the God of her fathers. By their understanding of this fact the prophets probed to the spiritual roots of the sin of popular religion, namely, its idolatrous nature. No matter what God was—or is—called, the "Man upstairs" or the God of Israel, who approved and encouraged man's every whim and desire, his nature was the same. He was a God who could be manipulated by men. Such a God was, of course, no God. His name simply camouflaged man's worship of himself. Outwardly relying upon the resources of a cult which centered its life in faith in God, the members of the religious community used their God as a tool to serve their own ends. Such a religion was exposed in its true light by the prophets and condemned as a sin and a sham.

For this reason they urged the people to abandon their false piety and to turn in faithfulness and obedience to the one true God through genuine repentance and righteousness. "If you truly amend your ways and your doings, if you truly execute justice one with another, . . . then I will let you dwell in this place." (Jer. 7:5, 7.) Without such thoroughgoing repentance the so-called faith of Israel and the religious acts which she performed would lead to disaster. The hoped for day of the Lord would be a day of dreadful disaster. God himself despised the faith which, however popular, presumed to use his power and authority to accumulate wealth unrighteously, to pamper lust, and to exalt the human creature above the Creator (Isa. 1:14). Every act of worship under these conditions was an abomination in his sight, even though it conformed externally to ancient tradition and practice (Amos 4:4-5; 5:21-24).

Popular religion in the time of Amos was easy, undemanding, and highly rewarding. Its failure lay in the blindness and perverseness of its adherents, who made no distinction between this comfortable cult of convenience and the true faith of Israel. In confronting this tragic complacency the prophets were moved to affirm again and again the transcendence of Israel's holy God and the radical nature of the moral-personal response which men must make to him, regardless of prudence, self-interest, and pride.

This view of the ancient prophetic attitude toward and treatment of popular religion prepares us as preachers to consider our own task in a period of "flourishing" faith. It is apparent that the desires and wants of men have multiplied greatly since the period of the prophets of Israel. It is also apparent that man still manipulates his religion in his quest for his desires. It is true he now has science and technology as his servants. Supplementing these, however, is his religion, which is also useful as his servant to do his bidding. Quite unconscious of his sin, the modern Christian readily identifies God and his kingdom with his own special interests, outlook, and hopes. He may view the Church as the custodian and defender of the faith which undergirds his economic or political philosophy or private concerns. To this tragic misunderstanding of the Church the preacher frequently contributes by preaching which misrepresents the gospel and misses the significance of the prophetic Word.

The preacher has one imperative obligation—to make known with fervor and conviction the independence of God and the ultimate authority of the One who subjects human motives and actions to the searching scrutiny of his holy will. More preaching on the theme of God as judge will restore to the gospel the moral quality which it once had in its biblical setting. Such preaching will also serve to identify plainly the ways of God so that they cannot be confused with the ways of man. The prophet must announce that only through judgment can the effect of God's redeeming love be known by society and by the individual.

Popular religion gains ground not only because it justifies and uncritically supports the plans of men but likewise because it comforts the anxious and the upset. It soothes the victims of the tensions produced by the rapid pace of modern living. Faith can quiet and calm the troubled soul and jangling nerves pretty much as a sedative in a capsule will do, and it will probably cost less! But the prophetic faith which is defined and proclaimed by the prophetic Word brings peace that is very costly. For it men must pay the price of humbling themselves, surrendering their desires and their hopes, and turning against the world in which they live. This is a peace which surrender to the God of infinite compassion and rigorous righteousness will give. It is not the peace gained by owning or trying to own the comforts of life or by degrading religion into an instrument of human desire. The prophetic Word will bring the peace of God to him who receives this Word humbly and sincerely. It will also bring serious conflict and struggle because it is set against every evil on every level of man's existence. It brings conflict into the world because of its unrelenting opposition to injustice among men. The man who hears this Word is summoned to witness to its meaning in the society in which he lives.

True prophetic preaching continuously sensitizes the hearer to the cries of the afflicted and the sorrow of the brokenhearted. So he is a man who is maladjusted to powerful forces in his world which have set themselves against the will of God. The peace which the hearer of such a Word has is a far cry from that of the happiness cults which pretend to derive their authority from the gospel. The prophet's task is so to preach as to keep himself and his people in constant tension with the world and to help them maintain a constant maladjustment to the evil that besets it. This he can do by affirming the primacy of doing justly and loving mercy in all human relations and in all institutional life. This he can never do by ignoring the evil that flaunts God's will and by mesmerizing his congregation through the repetition of pleasant sounds into believing that all is well.

In spite of the prophet's concern for ethical and social values which so often appears in his preaching, we ought not to think of him as a preacher of the so-called social gospel. While previous chapters on the passion, power, and perspective of the prophet dealt with this matter, illustrations of it in the sermons of the prophets will help the reader handle a very difficult question in his own preaching. Actually the prophet of Israel, even when addressing the nation or speaking to groups of people, spoke directly to the individual as well as to the entire community. His sermons, contrary to many preached today, were neither narrowly pietistic nor one-sidedly social in their aims and content. Instead they embraced the interests and needs of man as a person and as a member of society, comprehending these two emphases within the one gospel which the prophets so ardently preached.

In calling upon all men to seek the Lord and live, Amos was calling upon each man as well, knowing full well that repentance must originate in the humble spirit of the individual, even as it must result in the righteousness that exalts a whole nation. The summons to faith and obedience which the prophets so often sounded was to be received by each man in his solitariness, it is true; but it could have no real reception apart from man in his relations with others. So it was impossible for the prophets to preach the Word of the gospel simply as a solace for sick souls or only as a call to battle for sturdy crusaders who are eager to engage in the struggle for social justice. They were given the power to see that both souls and society were sick with a sickness that only God could heal.

When Jeremiah declared the meaning of the New Covenant (ch. 31), he was discussing the personal faith which would result from the revelation by God of his Word to men and their personal appropriation of its power in their lives. They would then be God's people, and he would be their God, forgiving their iniquity and remembering their sin no more. Surely this is a deeply personal faith of which Jeremiah spoke, a faith centered in the individual. Yet the prophet was speaking to the whole religious community rather than to any individual member of it. *They* would be God's people; *they* should all know him; he would forgive *their* iniquity.

The prophet certainly assumes here, even as he explicitly states elsewhere, that the covenant people are members one of another, called to practice justice and to show compassion. Personal salvation through the grace of God therefore calls for interpersonal relations based on a ministry of love. Personal peace, power, and joy are closely and inescapably associated with these relations, for God has made them inseparable. On the other hand, social justice, equitable treatment of minority groups, and the like cannot be attained apart from a profoundly personal devotion to the living God. This is true because God has determined the nature of man-in-community. The prophet handles the problem of the conflict between the individual and society by recognizing the function of the individual in the community of faith. From this community he derives the faith-centered meaning of his life. As he relates himself to it in faith, both share a common experience of redemption.

Some of the characteristic situations and problems which determined the content of the prophets' sermons have now been discussed. These included the meaning of nationhood, the witness of the suffering community of faith, and the nature of the true Church. The prophets preached also about social injustice, the use of strong drink, popular religion, and the tension between the social and the personal gospel. It is evident that their purpose was not primarily the solution of man's problems nor the amelioration of his lot. A reformer, social worker, or philanthropist can so love his fellow men as to work diligently to remove the evils that afflict them. This diligence, however, does not make him a prophet. One essential of true prophecy is to show the bearing of human situations upon the historically communicated will of God. It is his covenant will which the prophets proclaim and present as the guide to human behavior. The prophetic sermon exhorts men to do justly, to uphold the rights of the widow and orphan, to protect the poor farmer in his inheritance, to act honestly in the courts, to seek the ancient ways of mercy and goodness in the total life of the community. The true prophet has been anointed to proclaim liberty to the captives and to proclaim the acceptable year of the Lord.

But this is not his whole task; it is not even the most important part of it. This in itself is not prophetic preaching. What is distinctive and fundamental relates to something deeper than questions of freedom and justice. We find it in the preaching of Amos:

> You only have I known.
>
> .   .   .   .   .   .
>
> I sent among you a pestilence;
>
> .   .   .   .   .   .
>
> yet you did not return to me (3:2; 4:10) ;

in Hosea:

> I will say . . . ,
> "You are my people."

.   .   .   .

> I delight in piety, not sacrifice;
> And in the knowledge of God, rather than burnt-offerings.

.   .   .   .

> It is time to seek the Lord.

.   .   .   .

Therefore do you return to your God,

Practice kindness and justice. (2:23; 6:6; 10:12; 12:6 Amer. Trans.)

It appears also in Zechariah: "Not by might, nor by power, but by my Spirit, says the Lord of hosts" (4:6), and also in Isaiah:

By returning and resting shall you be saved,
In quietness and confidence shall be your strength (30:15 Amer:
    Trans.).

And in the preaching of the great prophet of the Exile, the same primary emphasis is made:

They that wait on the Lord shall renew their strength,
They shall mount on wings like eagles,
They shall run and not be weary,
They shall walk and not faint (Isa. 40:31 Amer. Trans.).

This is it—the only basis for a truly prophetic sermon. Pleas to do justly, to love mercy, are empty words apart from the plea to return to the living God. Life with him through faith and complete devotion alone makes possible the preservation of freedom, the reformation of society, and the establishment of justice in the world. To declare the passionate desire of God for the devotion of men, for their wholehearted faith and loyalty, to display his majesty and holiness that they may adore him and, adoring him, be restless until they rest in the acceptance of his commands, to magnify his name above all names so that every lesser allegiance may be brought into subjection to him—this is the essence of the true prophet's sermon, the reason for his denunciations and entreaties, for his fierceness and his occasional tenderness. This is the heart of all his utterances.

For this reason he vigorously and consistently attacks every kind of idolatry. For this reason he cries out God's demand for repentance and complete trust. For this reason he directs the fury of his word against every form of disloyalty. For this reason men listen to him as he brings the condemning yet forgiving presence of their Redeemer, without faith in whom they can have no hope in this life or in any other. Under the influence of such preaching the prophetic sermon becomes more than a sermon. It becomes a means of worship in which men see a vision of the true and living God, the everlasting King, the compassionate Savior, the Giver of the power to live faithfully and triumphantly. Here is preaching which is truly prophetic.

The contemporary preacher must bear the burden of announcing this redemptive Word whereby sinful men will be moved by God's Spirit to remember his lovingkindness toward them, to repent of their defiance of his will, and to resolve to live a new life based on his justice and his mercy. This new life demands renewal and direction, both with respect to its inwardness in the soul and in relation to its expression in the community, including both the Church and the social order in which it is set. To secure this result the prophet's proclamation will emphasize the nature of God and of his demands upon men. So the prophet will preach on theological themes, but largely as theology symbolizes in words the work of the redeeming God and the required response of his human creatures. His preaching will be concerned with the spiritual dynamics of the interaction between God and man rather than with theological reports as to the nature of each. To promote this interaction so as to make it effective in securing man's deliverance from sin is the proper purpose of the prophet's Word. The content of his message will always be a demonstration drawn from the drama of man's own history of the saving power of this divine Word. Thus the sermon will have a varied content which will always point to a single theme—the faithfulness of the God of faith, whom men must acknowledge as King of kings and Lord of lords.

The content of the prophetic proclamation is not the prophet's word but God's. The prophet must pray that the words of his mouth will be not only acceptable in the sight of God but also effective vehicles for bearing the redeeming Word of God with its power to search the heart, judge the conscience, and purify the desires of men. This Word centers in God's acts in history which it calls to the attention of men that they may be delivered from their bondage to sin and self. The sermon consists of the words whereby the prophet testifies to the nature of these acts and proclaims their continuing value for the salvation of all men. It is clear that this preaching is event-centered rather than idea-centered.

The prophet Samuel speaks these revealing introductory words to his people: "Now therefore stand still, that I may plead with you before the Lord concerning all the saving deeds of the Lord which he performed for you and for your fathers (I Sam. 12:7)." He goes on to tell how God brought Israel out of Egypt and into the Promised Land. Certain prophetic psalmists also stress the "saving events" of Israel's history: "I will call to mind the deeds of the Lord (Ps. 77:11)"; "we will . . . tell to the coming generation the glorious deeds of the Lord, . . . and the wonders which he has wrought (Ps. 78:4)"; "with my mouth I will proclaim thy faithfulness to all generations (Ps. 89:1)." And we hear the poignant words of God spoken through Amos:

> You only have I known
> of all the families of the earth (3:2).

His is an amazing assertion of the historical activity of God whereby he has "known" and loved his people in a special way. Since they perversely forgot this activity and love, the prophet must remind them of it.

This means that the prophet in the modern pulpit has no sermon apart from the message of the divine love which God has manifested in history. The Exodus, the entrance into Canaan, the Exile, the Restoration, the Incarnation, the Crucifixion, the Resurrection, and Pentecost—these are events initiated by God for the creation of the Church and the salvation of men. The gospel consists of the news of their occurring. Every aspect of preaching which is other than this is simply commentary and illustration for the sake of communicating it effectively to modern hearers. Consequently the content of the prophet's utterance can never be the prophet's reflections on the meaning of God or of sin or of the good life. What the prophet preaches is the good news of the God who acted in Jesus Christ and who acted also in and through Israel. God came to men again and again in judgment and in love, and finally in his Son. To declare that this coming has actually happened, why it happened, and its consequences for human life is the task of the prophet, who knows its meaning full well, for God has come to him with power. To report this coming and man's response to it is, of course, the principal purpose of Scripture. Thus the contemporary prophet is inevitably involved in biblical preaching.

Turning from a study of the nature and content of the prophetic proclamation, we should consider briefly the manner of this proclamation. In this connection it will be helpful to ask about the spirit and attitude of the prophet toward his task as these are set forth in the Bible and reflected in his preaching ministry. An idealization of the prophetic role may be detected in the book of Isaiah, for example, although other interpretations are certainly possible. Putting aside the question of the identity of the servant, we note reference to the qualities of tenderness (40:2), hopefulness (40:5), and boldness (40:9). The herald of good tidings is urged to lift up his voice with strength. The voice cries out: "Have you not known? Have you not heard?" (40:21.) This may be an allusion to past prophetic pronouncements on the subject of God's wonderful acts of deliverance in Israel's history.

In the servant poems one may find many suggestions which serve our purpose. These can be readily related to the spirit and attitude of the true prophet. The servant (prophet) is supported and chosen by God, whose spirit is in him. He seeks to secure international justice, he is gentle ("a dimly burning wick he will not quench"), and he will not fail or be discouraged until he has accomplished his task (42:1-4 *passim*). Whatever its author's meaning, Isa. 53 has great value when we apply its characterizations of the suffering servant to the ideal of a true prophet. The prophet may be called a man of sorrows, acquainted with grief, often rejected by men because he speaks of God's ways rather than theirs. He suffers for the sake of his people, yet mysteriously through this suffering demonstrates the redeeming love of his God.

This surely is the way of the true prophet who identifies himself with his people and with their sins and who preaches and lives vicariously for their deliverance. Isa. 61:1-2 reveals that God puts his Spirit within his servant (prophet), who then brings good tidings to the afflicted, binds up the brokenhearted, proclaims liberty to the captives and release to those in prison. The attitude of the prophet is that of one who seeks the salvation of men, and it is therefore one of radical optimism. The God whose will he proclaims is the God of righteous love. The

133

prophet is not a scold, who delights in saying unpleasant things to his sinful congregation. His awareness of their sin and his attack upon it must be understood within the framework of his faith in God. This God comes to men that they may have victory over sin and a new life of faithful obedience to their Redeemer.

We may now consider the style of the biblical prophets. This will aid in gaining further insight into their personalities and into their method of preaching as well. Since the prophetic books have not come down to us in the form of preaching manuals, they give us rather meager information about the technical aspects of effective preaching. Such matters as sermon preparation, the use of literary sources, the physical posture of the preacher, voice control, are only hinted at. Since we have at least portions of prophetic sermons, we may note their style and literary structure.

The reader is impressed by the simplicity and clarity of their style, even in English translation. Contrary to what is sometimes the case today, obscurity of thought and prolixity in the use of words do not describe the preaching style which the great prophets used. Where it is possible to strip from their original words the later editorial additions, we discover that they used short sentences packed with vivid, concrete terms and apt, readily recognized figures of speech. The strength of their feeling as well as a characteristic of the Hebrew tongue which they used is suggested by their simple, almost staccato style. Even in translation this may be noted: "Surely, he will do nothing,/the Lord God,/except he reveal his purpose to his servants the prophets./When the lion roars,/who does not fear?/When the Lord God speaks,/who will not prophesy? (Amos 3:7-8 Amer. Trans.)" And again: "For the vineyard of the Lord of hosts/is the house of Israel,/and the men of Judah/

are his cherished plantation;/he looked for justice,/but lo! bloodshed,/for righteousness,/but lo! a cry (Isa. 5:7 Amer. Trans.)." Sentences are short and to the point. Listeners do not have to wait for a long rush of words to come to an end before they can discover what has been said. There are plenty of exclamation points and periods, but few commas or semicolons, for there are few co-ordinate or subordinate clauses.

The sermon is usually poetic in structure or in spirit, so that the throbbing of the prophet's heart is reflected in the passionate rhythm of his words and measured cadences. Verbs are preferred to adjectives and adverbs. Fortunately for the prophet's dramatic and dynamic style, the latter are not common in Hebrew. Many imperative forms of the verb appear. The speaker seeks and commands action of mind and body. The short imperative verb form is suited to this need. We note "come, see, live, seek, go, choose, judge, come now, uphold, give ear, bring, hear, go up, behold, consider, be on guard, gather," and the like. Such words rather than abstract terms of general description serve to arrest attention, arouse interest, and secure a response.

Parables and other figures of speech are common. The prophets drew their language and imagery from the routine experiences of their people. They had no opportunity in their culture to learn elaborate creedal statements on which they might expatiate profoundly in the presence of their congregations after completing their studies and embarking upon their ministry. The parables of the vineyard, the pottery, the wine jars, the broken flask, the figs, the valley of dry bones, the two sticks, drew largely upon popular experience, as did the great number of references to familiar objects—the harlot, a wounded man, an ox, an ass, the bee (for Assyria), a mighty stream, shimmering summer heat, and the storm. There are also allusions to birds, plant life, sun, moon, eclipse, earthquake, clouds, mountains, and desert. There are similes, metaphors, the use of personification, hyperbole, and every other literary device which would promote vivid and effective speech.

The concrete, pungent, picturesque style of the prophetic preacher derives from the nature both of the Hebrew language which was his vehicle and of the message which he was required to communicate. He was not called to elucidate abstract truths about theology or the moral problem. Rather he was moved to be a prophet in order to announce God's action in history and the need for man's response. Into this announcement he put all his heart and mind and strength. The tensions of his actual historical situation drove him to forceful speech. It is not strange that the prophet met with a vigorous reaction when he preached. He was understood. There could be no inaction through doubt as to his meaning or misunderstanding of his words. With the concreteness and simplicity of his words we may compare the modern tendency toward wordiness in the pulpit. Does this betray the preacher's anxiety that he may not be speaking the needed word? Perhaps he keeps on speaking in the hope that he will stumble on it somehow.

In spite of differences in language, culture, and audience, the prophets of Israel can help the modern preacher in the important matter of the art of communication, even as they are indispensable in the essential matters which have been dealt with in preceding chapters. The effectiveness of these men of old in communication challenges our attention and demands our emulation. The preacher may profitably read the Bible to develop a style which will enable the Word that he utters to reach the people who are listening. If he is steeped in its vigorous, concrete, emotion-arousing words and in its simple yet exalted style, he cannot fail to reach his people, provided his vocabulary and thought are relevant to the life and need of his listeners. Personalities, events, tensions and conflicts in the community, recognized and important needs, and current behavior patterns of the group affect the consciousness of the preacher's hearers. His realization of this fact when he prepares his sermon will determine its "listenability" as far as style is concerned.

For true prophetic preaching there is one other kind of relevance which stands out prominently. The recognition and acceptance of this by the preacher will transform an interesting address into the living, redeeming Word of God, releasing men from sin and fear, and giving them peace and hope. This is the relevance of the eternal Word of deliverance to the predicament of men. This Word meets the deep human need for faith, forgiveness, courage, and meaningful living. It need not be obscured by complicated speculations or labored reflections on the metaphysical, philosophical, or theological implications of its meaning in the pulpit. When the preacher, himself one whom God has forgiven, simply declares that God so loved the world that he took action for each man in it, he has spoken to the heart of every person in his congregation in understandable language. Although he is baffled by the mystery of that love, the truth as to its reality he is bound to declare. Let him try to explain the mystery, but let him never forget to testify to the truth. If he is faithful to this obligation, he will be heard and understood.

VII

The Promise of Prophetic Preaching

THE MEANING OF THE TITLE OF THIS CHAPTER REQUIRES A BRIEF word of explanation. The word "promise" as used here does not mean primarily the possibilities which such preaching holds out for preachers, although these are not inconsiderable, but rather the note of confident hope which this preaching sounds as it declares the complete Word of the Lord. This question of promise or hope opens up one of the most critical questions of our time, both for the church and for those who in one way or another are affected by its program. This problem has been avoided studiously by many preachers. They self-consciously turn away from the Bible's vivid statements on the subject of hope, even while they diligently glean texts for sermons on justice and mercy in relation to the contemporary world. What is the truth about the prophetic approach to this matter? Can the true prophet avoid this phase of biblical teaching?

The easy dismissal of the biblical faith as this is expressed in the apocalyptic sections of the Bible is understandable. It is based in part on aversion to the crassly literalistic method of exegesis which so often characterizes its presentation. And in part it is due to a misunderstanding of the prophetic gospel.

This dismissal permits the more "positive" preaching message which is addressed to the needs of the present world on the supposition that this preaching will help produce the new order of justice and peace. Apocalyptic catastrophes, wars and rumors of wars, the upheaval of the earth, and the overthrow of civilization do not fit the modern preacher's neat pattern of historical development to which he relates the prophetic principles of righteousness and liberty. He still has some difficulty adjusting his thinking to the new fact, grimly manifested at Hiroshima, of the reality of catastrophe in the form of war and the upheaval of land and sea and civilization. Modern apocalyptic catastrophes may be fantastic, but their intrusion into the modern scene can hardly be ascribed to the fantasy of a deluded seer or the ravings of an overstimulated imagination which sees what isn't there. What the reality of calamity on a planetary scale means for his preaching, the modern preacher who seeks to be intelligent and reasonable finds it difficult to determine.

There is no doubt about the reality. Could Dante paint an Inferno which begins to compare with what was produced over Japan in earnest in 1945 and experimentally over Bikini subsequently? The prospect of world-wide destruction is now taken seriously. It is no longer viewed as the obsession of frustrated persons with twisted ideas about the Bible or with an inferiority feeling which will be removed when they witness the writhings of the victims of a world holocaust produced by an angry God. It doesn't require any elaborate biblical exegesis or logical argument to convince people in Hiroshima—survivors, that is—of the truth of the statement in Isaiah:

> See! the Lord is about to strip the earth, and lay it waste,
> Its surface he will distort.

. . . .

The earth will be stripped bare.

. . . .

The earth mourns, fades. (24:1, 3, 4 Amer. Trans.)

They would agree that the mirth of the world had gone, that all joy had reached its eventide. Indeed catastrophe, whether viewed as God's judgment or not, is a fact of dreadful experience; and hundreds of millions of men now live in fear of its intensified recurrence. This is the horrible fact and possibility with which men and women must now live daily.

How some Christian students of the Bible seize upon this evident confirmation of biblical teaching! These alarming events are the fulfillment of ancient biblical predictions; they show that the day of consummation is at last at hand and that destruction for the unbeliever will herald its coming. Driven by their fear and hope, many people throng to hear the prophets who accept this view of the Bible's teaching that they may learn the exact times and seasons and take all necessary precautions. No matter that other prophets, when faced by other crises in history, fixed other dates and seasons for the coming of the end and were discredited. This fate did not cure the ailment of modern man which these perennial peddlers of predictions so effectively exploit to their own advantage. History never ceases to bring its train of evils, and men never cease their effort to understand them in some ultimate sense. From the time of the false prophets who prophesied for hire to the present time of the crystal-ball gazer or the expert exegete of the book of Daniel, men have eagerly sought light and life beyond a world doomed to death and destruction.

We may regret this manipulation of the biblical texts for the purpose of catering to popular yearning for assurance about the future and treat the manipulators with some contempt. But

140

have we anything to take its place with which to heal the wounds caused by anxiety, uncertainty, and fear of the future? At the best, we can point out that certain biblical notions about coming events, while interesting, are simply survivals from a prescientific day. They have no relevance at all for men in a day of science and education. So the informed preacher is content to explain how these biblical ideas arose in early times in compensation for hardships and frustrations of various kinds. These biblical writers were, of course, mistaken; but we can forgive them, for they meant well. In the meantime men continue to be frightened, and their fear makes them do terrible things. Not the least of these is a kind of planning for the defense of their national communities which tends to bring about the very fate they fear—world-destroying war. What is the prophet's answer to the world's despair if the answer of the biblical literalist is rejected?

The literalist is discredited by the intelligent user of the Bible. The liberal who uses his Bible largely as one among many collections of sacred writings which have appeared in the history of mankind is helpless in this crisis. In the presence of newly discovered and fearful possibilities for human life which his concept of gradual human improvement never even hinted at his kind of Bible is worthless. And his preaching, insofar as it pertains to the Bible, is ineffective for his people and irrelevant to the tragedy of their situation. He tries to do his best, urging upon them the ethic of good will and love as somehow containing the meaning of history and the promise of mankind. But he is uneasy in the face of demonic forces which are spreading over the globe. He emasculates the Gospels of the New Testament by tearing from them the prophetic-apocalyptic element under the illusion that love in isolation from the total biblical gospel is enough. Wrath and judgment

141

belong to the Old Testament, love and hope to the New. So the promise is found exclusively in the latter—after its message has been mutilated.

The educated student of the Bible who is also a preacher of its gospel must conquer his prejudice toward the Bible's word of future hope by searching Scripture for its basic meaning and faith. If he does this, he will become aware of the truth of two realities—the truth of God and the truth of history. Once this is ascertained, a firm basis for hope can be found and the values in the approaches of the fundamentalist and the liberal can perhaps be reconciled. In the faith of the prophet God the Creator-Redeemer is both Judge and Savior. Only as Judge can he save, and only as Savior can he judge. These two roles are basically inseparable. In both parts of the Bible both wrath and love are found together. They express in their inter-relationship the redemptive activity of God.

At this point Christian people and their preachers, even while under the impression that they are dealing with the whole gospel, are guilty of distorting it grievously. The Word that the biblical prophet preaches is a word of wrathful love and of loving wrath. The poignant plea of Hosea's God is a moving account of the divine passion: "How can I give you up, O Ephraim!" (11:8). The sins of his people cannot continue unpunished, but God's love will never permit him to abandon them to destruction. The prophet who preaches today must remember that the redemption which God's love desires for us men requires the judgment which our sin demands. We may ask how this twofold response of God to his human creatures is exhibited in the processes of history. Is the meaning of the history the awful consequences of which we now so terribly fear related to both the righteousness and the compassion of God? May we hope, when wrath seems on the verge of crushing

142

everything we hold dear in a technological, atomic, fear-ridden age?

There was also a kind of technology as well as suffering and fear in the days of the prophets. There was also a view of history which was an integral part of the prophets' faith. By reason of this they could hope on even when their world was tumbling down over their heads. The early writer in the book of Genesis antedates the writing prophets but anticipates their understanding of history. There at the beginning of history was the Garden of Eden, where simple comradeship between a man and his wife and trusting obedience to God their Creator were the marks of peace and joy. Then came an upheaval. Man used his God-given freedom to defy his Maker. He proceeded to create civilization, building cities and inventing things as a mark of this defiance. This work of his brain and brawn was rejected by an outraged God because it signified self-worship and flagrant idolatry. So the rains descended, the flood came, and most of civilization was wiped out. This is the view of the great prophets. The arrogance of the human creature which he manifests by adoring the work of his hands and the product of his tools severs him from his Redeemer and thus from the true source of his life. Judgment is then unavoidable.

For the prophets history is thus the scene of God's action, the theater where is enacted the mighty historical drama of judgment and deliverance. On its stage God chooses a single people and works to make them a holy nation, which will one day draw all nations to it in response to its faithful portrayal of the glory of its God. God controls events in order to fulfill his purpose of redemption. So time is eventful rather than simply chronological. It is God's time and must be measured by the various actions which God takes to put his plans into effect. It is the history of salvation and only incidentally the history of wars and human struggle. Its turning points are not treaties, battles, or the appearance of great leaders. They are rather the gift of the covenant, the choice of a people, the call of the prophets, and the disciplinary punishment of God's people through historical forces and circumstances. At any moment each man and nation stands in the middle of such a history, no matter what his human role, whether it be that of a politician, military leader, or social reformer.

Disaster in this biblical view of history is God's way of directing history on the path of redemption. Its judgments further this purpose, although not always in an obvious way. Without judgment men cannot come to the faith and repentance which brings them finally to God in full surrender. But without divine love the judgment is futile and becomes simply an exhibition of senseless destruction and meaningless misery. When history is interpreted in this manner, it does not end in a blind alley. It moves toward an end, an end which is determined by the power of the God who controls his world and who loves its inhabitants.

Here we see the part that creation plays in the historical process. It signifies not only the contingency of the world and nature, but also their instrumental function in constituting the scene of the great drama and one of the means for bringing it to fruition. Nature is used by its God, and it can never conquer or defeat his purposes at the last. Even its evil aspects are turned into good by the Redeemer of men. This is the basis for the prophetic hope which shines in the darkness of a God-defying, power-worshiping world. Evil cannot have the last word because God lives! This is the profound meaning of history from the standpoint of biblical prophetic faith.

This truth should make it clear that there can be no judgment without hope also, unless God cancels all that he has promised to his people. History is his, and it moves in the direction which he has set. But it does not do this mechanically or consistently, for the freedom of his creatures and the completeness of his control over nature are not yet fully manifest. Implicit in the preaching of the prophets is the belief that the days are coming when all men will know God and gladly serve him in peace and justice. Some of the prophets make this point explicit. Nations will beat their swords into plowshares, and they shall learn war no more. A transformation of the earth will include the regeneration of men. There will be a highway of rejoicing over which God will bring the redeemed; and sorrow and sighing will flee away, never to return. So history moves on to its wonderful climax for men of faith and good will. The people to whom the prophets preached wanted this fulfillment without the conditions attached to it. The day of the Lord was desired, but the righteous demands of the Lord for repentance and obedience were rejected. They failed to realize that history's glorious consummation required full compliance with the will of history's God. Without this there could be no hope.

The true prophetic preacher, called by the God of mercy and dedicated to the task of announcing the centrality of man's deeply personal and spiritual relation to him as the source of life, is bound to have hope and to preach it. The meaning of the biblical idea of resurrection, which inevitably proceeds from this prophetic teaching, relates directly to the prophetic view of history, since it represents its fulfillment for the individual and for the community of faith. The development of the prophetic promise comes to a sharp focus in the apocalyptic writings of the Bible. The promise is complete and unreserved life with God, joy in his presence, strength through his power, and love because he first loved us. This promise was bound to triumph over death and to give the assurance of life eternal in community and in devotion to the God of history, whose way is justice and whose will is peace. So the apocalyptic fulfillers of the prophetic Word—or rather the interpreters of its full meaning—could declare with deep assurance that

> He will destroy death forever.
> So the Lord God will wipe away tears
> From every face. (Isa. 25:8 Amer. Trans.; Rev. 21:3-5.)

The meaning of this triumphant word of victory over death has too often been divorced from the faith of the prophets, who declared its essential nature even though they lacked the equipment to describe it in terms of life beyond the grave. Preacher and layman alike tend to confuse the nature of their Christian hope as their thinking swings, on the one hand, to an emphasis upon "prophetic" social justice in this life and, on the other, to the idea of some kind of disembodied ethereal existence in the other world. The prophetic promise is the complete redemptive Word of God rather than a set of social principles guaranteed to bring peace and prosperity to all men. This Word comprises the *total* purpose of God to realize his plans for his creatures in spite of evil, sin, and death. Such a realization will mean the preservation forever of the values which God cherishes and of the persons-in-community whom he loves with an everlasting love. So the one who hears this prophetic Word and does it, no matter how unimpressive the effect of his obedience to it, may be sure that it counts in the divine economy. He may have confidence that his passionate devotion to the achievement of a better human community ultimately makes a difference both for him and for his fellows.

How empty may be the words of the preacher who is content

to be largely a spokesman of good causes aiming at social betterment! We spend a century in a Christian mission in China, and
our work of social amelioration and evangelism is suddenly
snatched from our hands. We become eager members of peace
organizations and preachers of the gospel of the Prince of
Peace, then our world blows up in our faces. The dread of a
war of appalling proportions haunts us day and night. What
shall the prophet preach in such a time as this? Support of the
United Nations? A rejection of colonialism wherever and for
whatever reason it still exists? More and more intelligent economic aid for needy nations? Yes, all this and more too. Above
all he will preach that the labors of dedicated men who love
their fellows of whatever race or clime and their God will not
be in vain. Of such devotion and toil is the kingdom of heaven.

A prophetic preacher cannot be content to point to the resurrection hope once a year. This is to reduce it to the vanishing
point, out of an almost perverse forgetfulness that it is really
the whole gospel, the clue to the complete Word of salvation
for men. Neither may he, no matter how often he preaches on
the theme, destroy its true meaning by leaving out of account
its prophetic realism. This establishes for the Christian hope
meaningful moral content, social significance, and concreteness for persons who prize their self-consciousness, their will
to be and to live, and their association with their fellows.

Preaching of this kind is true to the faith of the Hebrew
prophets, although they failed to express their hope in terms
of resurrection. They possessed the important ingredients of
this hope in their evaluation of men as sons of God, of life as
spiritual and moral communion with him, and of society as
potentially the community of the redeemed who are faithful
and obedient to their Lord. Although they had no concept
with which to symbolize a belief in victory over death for the

individual, their beliefs contained the essential meaning of life eternal. What is this life except a life equipped with the power of God for creative living on the personal and social levels and motivated by a deep desire to share it with others? It is this life which preachers must preach and exemplify, for it is this life which identifies for the Christian the kind of hope that has ethical and personal and final validity. This is the hope which drives men into heroic struggles for freedom and peace on earth in the name of the God who is both the joy of earth and the hope of heaven.

How in heaven's name can preachers avoid this mighty theme of prophetic hope then and devote their time to discussing from their pulpits burning social questions of the day? Can the prophetic preacher ignore the intimate relationship of these questions to the prophetic gospel of the Christ who lived and died and lived again? Such a prophetic hope is the true Christian hope. It is what the souls of stricken, fear-ridden men plead for, even though inaudibly. This is the prophetic promise, and this is the great theme of prophetic preaching as well as its powerful motive. And this is the prophetic Word of promise and hope which became flesh and dwelt among men, even Jesus Christ our Lord.

The man who preaches like the prophets of old is the man who has been called by the Man of Galilee and who knows that in him is the prophetic Word in all its power and splendor. When he preaches the gospel which is Christ, he does it with the passion of a devotion which has captured his heart and mind. As he understands the meaning of this call in relation to the prophetic Word and to the world for whose salvation the Word was sent, he knows more profoundly the implications for his ministry of the "fulness of the Godhead bodily" (Col. 2:9 K.J.V.) . Aroused in heart and mind and soul by the Christ who has confronted and called him, he finds released within him new sources of power whereby he can more adequately proclaim the Word of redemption. He is encouraged and strengthened to carry on his difficult ministry by the power which has come to him from without, but which is strangely and wonderfully his own possession. Thus the Spirit of his Lord enables him to declare the fact and the meaning of the prophetic Word to people desperately needing it yet fearfully rejecting it.

Christ is also the perspective of the prophetic preacher. The viewpoint, the faith, and the relation to the world which characterized the prophets of old and may do so today are supremely illustrated in the person and work of Jesus Christ, since he *is* the prophetic Word. And the modern prophet who has received this Word and for whom to live and preach is Christ has the purpose which was Christ's. With both love and wrath the Christ of God performed his deeds and uttered his words for a single purpose—that men might turn to the God who had sent him and thus enter his kingdom. When he was no longer in the flesh, through the gift of his Spirit his prophets were filled with the same consuming purpose. They witnessed to what they has seen and heard, to the action of God in sending his Son to save the world, to that Son's life and ministry, to his death and resurrection, whereby men of faith might find new life and new power. This was the essence of their preaching, which represented the fulfillment of the redemptive Word of God and its complete expression among men. We may reread each of the foregoing chapters in this book and substitute the name of Christ for such terms as the redemptive Word of God or the prophetic Word and find that the substitution fits much of the context.

The prophetic Word is the incarnate Word of the Fourth Gospel and of the Christian faith, which was in the beginning with God and which was in various ways made known to the prophets. All that Christ is and means to men as Lord, Savior, Redeemer, Friend, Messiah, Comforter, Judge, Holy Spirit, is expressed when the full meaning of the prophetic Word is declared. He is the Word of God and of the prophets, whom we must preach lest we betray our calling. This Word is divine justice, righteousness, love, personal, regenerative, spiritual power. It is the dynamic for society's redemption, the source of our faith, the meaning of our lives, and the promise of our destiny. So to preach the Word of the prophets, we must preach Christ, in the wide and profound sense in which the prophetic preacher's task has been outlined in this study.

Index of Scripture References

151

Index of Subjects

153

Commitment, 14, 23, 26, 98, 107, 113
Communication, 39, 41, 42, 65, 74, 84, 136
Communism, 51, 52
Community: chosen, 82; economic, 91; eternal life in, 146; of faith, 113; national, 109, 111; political, 116; of the redeemed, 147; religious, 122; suffering, 127
Compassion, 16, 23, 41, 59, 76, 94, 125, 127, 142
Condemnation, 41, 72, 76, 88, 96, 101, 116, 122
Confession, 35, 55, 114
Congregation (s), 28, 34, 55, 62, 83, 91, 102, 114, 125, 134, 137
Conscience, 36, 46, 53, 55, 72, 73, 79, 92, 95, 122, 131
Corruption, 23, 46, 72, 88, 116
Court, 58
Covenant, 57, 62, 69, 86, 102, 103, 107, 109, 127, 144
Creation, 74, 94, 100, 101
Creation of the Church, 132, 144
Creator, Redeemer, 22, 77, 100, 103, 123, 143
Creature (s), 99, 100, 123, 130, 142, 146
Creed, 59, 62, 91
Crucifixion, 132
Cult (s), 61, 62; fertility, 87, 122; of happiness, 125
Culture, 32, 36, 41, 43, 45, 72, 73, 81, 84, 89, 91, 118, 135, 136
Curses from God, 36

Damascus, 109
Dancing, 77
Daniel, 140
Dante, Inferno, 139
Day of the Lord, 53, 121, 123, 145
Death, 25, 41, 62, 80; of Christ, 97, 140; of the Son, 149; triumph over, 146, 147
Dedication, 14, 29, 77, 107, 121
Deliverance, 53, 54, 82, 92, 97, 98, 110, 130, 137, 143

Demonic, 141
Destiny, 17, 33, 40, 113
Devotion, 13, 14, 23, 24, 26, 28, 62, 120, 121, 129, 146, 148
Disaster, 22, 72, 123
Doom, 21, 67, 72, 110, 117
Drink, intoxicating, strong, 119, 120, 127
Drunkards, 24

Economic aid, 147
Ecstasy, 21
Edomites, 51
Education, 73, 81, 90, 141
Egypt, Egyptians, 33, 51, 57, 60, 131
El, 74
Elijah, 59, 116
Elohim, 74
Encounter, 92, 94
Episcopacy, 45
Eternal, the, 17, 72, 148
Ethic (s), 23, 58, 59, 72; Christian, 97; of good will, 141; humanistic, 81
Evangelism, 147
Evangelist, 121
Evil, 13, 16; national, 25, 36, 51, 58, 75, 98, 110; social, 23, 116, 118, 119, 125, 144, 146
Exile, 97, 113, 129
Exiles, 112, 113, 132
Exodus, 97, 132
Ezekiel, 14, 17, 26, 48, 68, 75, 108

Faith, 19, 25, 30, 34, 36, 40, 41, 49, 51, 53, 55, 57, 58, 68, 77, 88, 93, 102, 108, 113; day of, 121; God of, 131; need for, 137; personal, 126; prophetic, 144, 145, 146, 150
Faithfulness, 40, 41, 42, 76, 102, 123, 131
False prophets, 18, 44, 45, 69, 140
Family, 33, 40, 77, 94, 101
Farm, 17
Farmer, 16, 61, 110, 116
Fertility, 87
Fertility cult, 94

154

Index of Subjects

Figures of speech, 134, 135
Flood, 143
Foreign policy, 29, 105
Forgiveness, 26, 54, 88, 115, 137
Four Roses, 46
Freedom, 22, 24, 36, 37, 74, 76, 90, 100, 102, 103, 128, 129, 143, 145, 148
Fundamentalist, 142

Garden of Eden, 143
Gaza, 109
Genesis, 143
Germany, 109
God: activity of, 19, 29, 30, 149; angry, 139; in Christ, 99; compassionate, 23, 59, 145; covenant, 18, 22, 57, 69, 72, 120; of the fathers, 17, 72; and goddess, 87; goodness of, 71, 73, 96, 99, 138; of history, 112, 146; of Israel, 13, 15, 25, 86; judge, 142; life with, 145; living, 29, 58, 61, 94, 95, 112, 129; righteous, 35, 61; of salvation, 22; self-disclosure of, 23, 73; supreme, jealous, 121; the Wholly Other, 22
Gods, 88, 90
Gods, secular, 91, 94
Gomer, 61
Goodness of God, 71, 73, 96, 99, 138
Gospel, 18, 27, 56, 59, 62, 70, 80, 91; definition of, 132; the Fourth, 149; of the Prince of Peace, 147; prophetic, 138; of salvation, 92, 102, 104, 108, 112, 114, 120; social, 125; social and personal, 127; the whole, 142; Word of, 126
Gospels, 141
Government, 23, 58, 90
Grace, 30, 39, 52, 57, 80, 127
Greek philosophy, 40

Habakkuk, 31, 50
Hebrew (s), 85, 88
Hebrew language, 135, 136
Herdsman, 15
Hezekiah, 67
Hierarchy, 77

Hiroshima, 139
History: acts in, 131, 136; climax of, 145; crises in, 140; Lord of, 15; meaning of, 74; purpose in, 114; of religions, 21; turn of, 29; view of, 143
Holiness, 15, 23, 25, 75, 94, 99, 115, 122, 129
Holy, 16, 22, 55, 94, 98, 99, 121, 123
Hope, 39, 72, 80, 101, 121, 130, 137, 138, 140, 142, 144, 145; Christian, 146, 147; of heaven, 148
Hosea, 14, 16, 26, 35, 40, 60, 61, 67, 83, 87, 90, 94, 119, 128, 142

Ideologies, 36, 52
Idolatry, 51, 115, 130
Idols, 69
Image: of God, 77; of man, 99, 100
Imperialism, 33
Incarnation, 53, 132
Individual, 13
Individuality, 22, 71, 73, 101, 103, 104, 105, 124, 126, 127, 145, 148
Industry, 86
Injustice, 15, 34, 51, 110, 116, 118, 122, 125
Integrity, 31, 69
Intelligence, 67, 69, 81
Interaction between God and man, 130
International, 26, 40, 49, 105, 108, 133
Isaiah, 14, 15, 16, 22, 24, 25, 34, 35, 37, 47, 48, 54, 61, 86, 94, 117, 118, 119, 133, 139
Israel, 13, 20, 25, 45, 49, 57, 72, 85; economy of, 87; God of, 92; history of, 133; out of Egypt, 131; religious leaders of, 111

James, William, 68
Japan, 139
Jeremiah, 13, 14, 17, 22, 24, 25, 26, 46, 47, 54, 61, 67, 69, 75, 94, 118, 126
Jerusalem, 16, 25, 37, 40, 48, 112
Jesus Christ, 43, 59, 132, 148, 149

Salvation, 22, 41, 42, 47, 54, 55; -history, 57, 59, 62, 69, 79, 80, 92, 94, 97, 98, 99, 103, 104, 105, 106; history of, 143; personal, 127, 131, 132, 133; word of, 147, 148
Samaria, 15
Samuel, 25, 131
Sanctuary, 58, 61
Saul, 75
Savior, 23, 53, 59, 104, 130, 142, 150
Second Isaiah, 112, 113, 115
Secularism, 89
Self, sin and, 131
Self-righteousness, 122
Self-worship, idolatry of, 143
Selfhood, 100, 120
Sensuality, 16, 47, 61, 118, 119, 120
Servant, 23, 113, 133; poems, 133; suffering, 133
Sex, cult of, 89
Sexual intercourse, 87
Sin, 15, 19, 33, 38, 40, 48, 52, 54, 55, 63, 64, 75, 83, 95, 99, 100; bondage to, 131, 132, 134, 137, 146; confession of, 114; overt, 101, 104, 106; of pride, 122, 123, 124
Sinai, 22
Sinner (s), 24, 30
Sinner, forgiven, 82, 100, 101
Society, 23, 24; reformation of, 129; sick, 126; tribal, 85, 101, 103, 115, 117, 124, 125
Social: betterment, 147; concern, 31; evil, 61, 116; institution, 63; justice, 146; order, 116, 130; practices, 39; pressure, 95; principles, 146; process, 33, 73; questions, 118, 148; reformers, 70, 86, 144; relations, 43; situation, 68; trends, 49, 88; unrest, 86; values, 117, 125
Solomon, 60
Son of God, 100, 132, 149
Sons of God, 147
Speech, 92, 95, 134, 135, 136
Spirit, 28, 36, 39, 48, 49, 74, 75, 76,

Spirit—cont'd
77, 78, 79, 80, 121, 126, 130, 133, 149
Spirit, Holy, 150
Spirituality, 28
Spokesman, 14, 22, 42, 47, 48, 55, 59, 82, 84, 91, 147
State, 25
State, department of, 61, 90, 111
Style, 134, 135, 136, 137
Subversion, 25, 51
Succession, prophetic, 28
Suffering, 27, 71; obedient, 114, 115, 143; servant, 113
Surrender, 22, 26, 30, 125
Sycamore-fig trees, 15
Syria, 109

Teaching, teacher, 56, 57, 59, 62, 114, 138, 145
Temperance, 120, 121
Temple, 15, 121, 122
Temptation, 35
Theocracy, 25
Theology, biblical, 92, 93, 99, 103, 130
Tongues, 77
Tradition (s), 25, 57, 73, 97, 102, 123
Trust, 78, 130
Truth, 39, 41, 43, 68, 94, 97, 137, 142

United Nations, 147
Uzziah, 15

Vision (s), 46, 48, 68, 70, 71, 75, 97
Vocabulary, relevant, 136
Voice, 19, 21, 79

Watchman, 49, 51, 52
Watchtower, 50
Whiskey, 66
Wife, 26, 143
Will, 24, 30, 39, 53, 72, 80, 94, 97, 102, 104; covenant, 128; God's holy, 124; righteous, 111, 115, 120, 121

Index of Subjects

Wine, 61, 89, 90, 119, 120
Wisdom, 68, 76
Wise men, 24
Witness, 30, 55, 79
Word, 14, 20, 28, 30, 40, 42; Christ as, 149; complete, 138; divine, 131; of God, 146; healing, 83; incarnate, 149; made flesh, 43; preaching of, 82; revealed, 71; of salvation, 69; saving, 92; sent, 148
World, 28, 29, 75, 82, 103; nations of, 114; out of, 115; redemption, 114; relation to, 149; tumbling down, 143
World War II, 109
Worship, 38, 56, 62, 87, 94, 99, 102, 104, 120, 121; means of, 130; self-, 122, 123
Wrath, 16, 34, 36, 41, 75, 105, 116, 141, 142, 149

Zechariah, 129
Zion, 110, 112